Music Makers

Music circle times to include everyone

by
Dr Hannah Mortimer

Illustrated by
Robyn Gallow

A QEd Publication

First published as the *Music Makers Approach* in 2000 by NASEN
Revised edition published in 2006

© Hannah Mortimer

ISBN 1 898873 48 8

British Library Cataloguing
A catalogue record for this book is available from the British Library.

Published by QEd Publications, 39 Weeping Cross, Stafford ST17 0DG
Tel: 01785 620364
Fax: 01785 607797
Website: www.qed.uk.com
Email: orders@qed.uk.com

Printed in the United Kingdom by J.H. Brookes (Stoke-on-Trent).

Contents

Introduction

Why music?

Music is an amazing thing. It stills a crying baby. It captures a toddler's attention. It holds the interest of children who, in any other situation, might be experiencing considerable learning or communication difficulties. It provides opportunities for even very young children to join together sociably in a group, long before they are old enough to attend an early years setting. It encourages children who find it hard to move, to move more freely. It helps parents and carers share pleasure and form closer attachments with their young children. It encourages children who do not like to look and to listen to do just that. And, above all, it is fun.

As such a powerful tool it is not surprising that music can be used very effectively to teach young children to learn and to develop. In this book you will be helped in Chapter 1 to develop a regular music session as part of your early learning activities or play sessions. Not only will this become a useful way of working towards the Early Learning Goals for the foundation stage of learning (*Curriculum guidance for the foundation stage*) or within the *Birth to three matters* framework (*Birth to three matters: A framework to support children in their earliest years*), but you can use it to welcome and include children with a wide range of special needs. You should also find that the targets map easily onto the *Early Years Foundation Stage* (EYFS) framework. You can use it as a regular feature of your toddler group or Sure Start session. You can also adapt the activities if you are a childminder, if you are working with older children, or if you are planning your sessions within a special school.

Inclusive education

You will have heard a great deal over the past few years about inclusion and about planning activities that suit everyone, regardless of their needs or disabilities. This musical approach puts these ideas into practice. It encourages you to provide *inclusive* activities which suit *all* the children, regardless of age and stage. Therefore the activities should be flexible enough both to match admirably the needs of the older children as they prepare for starting school, but also all children who are still very young or who have special educational needs.

The Music Makers project

Several years ago, I started a regular developmental music group at a child development centre as part of the multidisciplinary service for pre-school children with special needs. Parents joined us from all around with the excellent support of the voluntary transport service. These sessions were much enjoyed by the children, but also became a useful way of teaching them new developmental milestones, using music as the attention-getter and motivator. This makes the sessions rather different from *music therapy* where children are encouraged to respond and express themselves through the therapeutic medium of music. In *developmental music therapy*, music simply becomes the tool used to teach developmental steps.

We asked the parents and therapists already working with the children to provide us with an idea of what each child could do, and to mark particular targets they would like the child to achieve through attending the group. This is a similar approach to the one you will read about in Chapter 3, and the assessment we used is similar to that you will be using on page 14. We were delighted with how the children responded, and the parents and carers were keen to see the groups continue. However, for some of them, it was a long way to travel with a small child.

With the help of a grant, we were able to provide satellite groups around the area. This enabled many pre-school playgroups to become trained in the approaches so that, week by week, they could take over the running of a group and welcome any local children with special needs who were able to join them. All the materials and approaches were collected together in a book to support those early years educators taking part in the project. This book is the result.

Requirements of the SEN Code of Practice

Registered foundation stage providers need to have regard to *The Special Educational Needs Code of Practice* (DfES, 2001), and this book suggests one approach for designing individual education plans to suit children with special needs. The procedure is explained in simple and practical terms, again using musical activities as a vehicle for teaching your targets, but with suggestions for helping the children generalise the skills learned into the rest of their play. Even for children who are not yet three, you can follow this approach and plan individual targets for children with additional needs.

You will be helped to share your approaches with the family, and you will also be led through a form of assessment and record-keeping which you can use to gather baseline information, set targets, and record progress. There are also suggestions for liaising with other professionals who might be involved. All this you will find in Chapter 3.

The Early Learning Goals, *Birth to three*, and the EYFS framework

Some of you may be working in a registered foundation stage setting and therefore following the framework of the foundation stage curriculum (QCA). Because the activities suggested are designed to be inclusive for all children, you will be able to use them to plan learning outcomes for children working towards the Early Learning Goals. Each activity is cross-referenced to the Early Learning Goal it contributes towards, and the key used is given on page 69. You will be helped to plan your activities and to provide evidence of your planning ready for inspection. You will also be helped to adapt each activity flexibly to suit your older children and also those who might need additional help or a less challenging approach. If you are working within the *Birth to three* framework, you will also find that each activity is cross-referenced to page 72. The joy of using a musical approach is that the same activities can be relevant to children at many different ages and stages. This approach adapts well, therefore, to the new Early Years Foundation Stage – all the targets should map easily onto the new EYFS framework.

Different settings

You are likely to be doing your musical activities in a whole range of different settings. Some of you might be starting a regular music slot as part of your existing early years session; some in nursery classes or schools; in assessment nurseries or special schools; in social services family centres; in parent and toddler groups; in health centres; or in childminding groups. We have used the approach in all of these settings, including groups for parents and toddlers where there are particular challenges in managing the children's behaviour. We have found the approach especially helpful in Sure Start groups. Here, the children are helped to develop attention, language and social skills and the adults are given ideas for taking home that help to build their attachments to their children. You will find more suggestions about this in *RUMPUS*, *Making Connections* and *Music and Play* published by QEd Publications. In all these cases, the activities provided a useful tool for encouraging the children to join in co-operatively in a group, to look and listen for instructions, and, above all, to share fun and pleasure with the adults in their lives.

There is nothing new or specialist about the activities. Each one should feel utterly familiar and practicable. This book helps you use these very familiar activities in a structured and planned way, and to maintain important evidence that you are setting out to meet special educational needs and to work towards the Early Learning Goals or to plan activities within the *Birth to three* framework.

Involving parents and carers

Hopefully the parents who come to your group will have been sharing musical moments with their children long before your musical activities were begun. Research tells us just how important early lap play and nursery songs and rhymes are to the developing child's two-way communication, language, and even later reading skills. We also know how important early communication and nurturing is for developing positive attachments and mental health. Do involve parents and carers fully. This book will share ideas for involving parents and families in the music groups and extending the activities to home.

Make a special welcome to parents in your neighbourhood who might have a young child with SEN or additional needs. It does not matter if they do not belong to your setting. Why not tell your health visitor that you are starting a Music Makers group and that you would welcome young visitors with additional needs? Local families could then join your session for the half-hour music group, and have the opportunity to get to know other parents in their area.

It does not matter about the child's age either. These activities have been successfully used in groups of mixed age pre-school children from babyhood to rising five and beyond. Why not invite parents and younger siblings to join the session once you are confident and use it as a useful introduction to pre-school for your future customers?

Keeping records

In these times of accountability we are becoming increasingly used to keeping records – records of activities, records of planning, records of your individual assessments, records of progress and 'added value'. The assessment and record-keeping sheets on page 73 will come as no surprise, but, in order to be useful, need to fit in with what you are already required to do. For those of you in schools or registered settings and following the foundation stage curriculum, you will find that each activity is linked to the Early Learning Goals, the *Birth to three* framework and to the assessment target for any child with additional needs. Hopefully, this cross-referencing will be a useful aid as you prepare your record-keeping both for inspection and for meeting the requirements of the *SEN Code of Practice*. The approach will adapt easily to the new EYFS framework.

How to use this book

When we trained colleagues in the project, they were introduced to the chapters stage by stage in order gradually to become familiar with the approach, and to plan more and more of the music session themselves without the trainer's help. This 'step-by-small-step' approach is already familiar to those of you who are used to developmental teaching. If you are planning a Music Makers group, start small and gradually build up your activities as you become more confident. You will find a session planning sheet on page 75 to help you. You will find the activities collected in Chapters 4 to 9 will fit with the sections on the session planning sheet. This will enable you to plan a balanced session and also to include activities to meet particular needs or cover particular Early Learning Goals.

You will not need to be proficient on a musical instrument as a cassette recorder and tapes can be used instead. Others might like to revive old skills on a guitar or keyboard and you will find the resource list on page 11 helpful. All of you need to practise your singing. It is only by doing it that it gets better. Even if you sing out of tune, learn to do it with confidence and style! It is your enthusiasm rather than your proficiency that will encourage the children to join in. And singing *does* improve the more you do it.

Chapter 1

Getting ready for music

A range of situations

We have incorporated Music Makers successfully into all of the following:

- 'Bump and New arrivals' clubs – a mixture of mothers at late pregnancy and in the first few months of motherhood learning and sharing lap rhymes and musical moments.

- Post-natal support groups in health centres along with older siblings.

- As part of the session at 'drop in' centres within Sure Start schemes (for example, see *Music and Play* groups, QEd Publications).

- Carer and Baby groups – music for 'Sitters, Standers and Explorers' (this is the terminology in the *Birth to three matters* framework for children 8 to 18 months).

- Carer and toddler groups – groups for parents and children around 18 to 24 months (known as 'Movers, Shakers and Players' in the framework).

- Pre-school and playgroup sessions.

- Child development centres.

- Parents' groups for encouraging their child's early development (for example, see *Step by Step* groups, QEd Publications).

- NHS Groups for parents and children focusing on how to manage difficult behaviour (for example, see *RUMPUS* groups, QEd Publications).

- NHS Groups for parents and children focusing on improving attachments and relationships (for example see *Making Connections* groups, QEd Publications).

- Nursery classes and groups.

- Nursery and KS1/2 classes in special schools.

- Foundation stage and KS1 classes.

- Out of school care groups.

- Holiday schemes.

- Childminder cluster groups.

- Home groups.

What you will need

When you decide to start a music group, you will need to start collecting musical instruments, and you will find suggestions for these below. You can usefully build this into a project on music or sound, helping the children to make a range of percussive and shaking instruments themselves. You will also need some musical accompaniment. Perhaps you can harness some local musical talent and encourage a neighbour, fellow teacher or parent to play the piano for you, a guitar, or fund-raise for an electronic keyboard. If not, a cassette recorder and tapes or a CD-player can work well. Make sure the quality of sound is good, and have one adult on stand-by to manage the machine so that the group leader does not need to worry about it. You will need to take time before the session to ensure all the tapes are the right way round and at the correct place.

Choose tapes, CDs and accompaniments which are simple and not drowned out with too much background sound and jazzy harmonies; the children need to hear the tune line. Look for tapes and sound-tracks which represent all the richness of our multi-cultural society. You might be able to record a pianist playing, or ask someone with a strong voice to put favourite songs on tape for you. Some of the activities suggest particular tunes and tapes which you might find useful (see page 76 for resource suggestions).

You will also need a suitable area of the premises or hall to hold the group in. A large hall is fine so long as you use chairs to signal to the children where to sit and arrange them in a circle facing the leader. The leader should sit at the end of the circle nearest the wall so that the children are facing away from the attraction of the large space in the remainder of the hall. This way, they are less inclined to run around. Alternatively, you can have a circle of chairs for adults around the edge and a 'song carpet' in the centre of the ring for the children to sit on, also in a circle.

We have held other groups successfully on the story mat of a playroom or class. The idea is to define the boundary clearly (a mat or a chair shows the children just where to sit) and to have all the children and adults able both to face each other and the leader; hence the idea of the circle. Young children and some of those who have additional needs may well wish or need to sit next to a parent or adult, or on a parent's knee. In the groups we hold in child development centres, we all sit on the floor in a large circle; parents, children, siblings, therapists, leader and all. Smaller groups have worked successfully as home groups.

How to organise your music session

Use the session planning sheet on page 75 to help you plan the activities, aiming for twenty minutes to half an hour's duration.

First choose a well-known favourite to signal the beginning of a session and become your 'theme tune'. *If you're happy and you know it* involves actions and familiar words, is easy to pick up, and seems to be liked by most children. Other favourites could be *The wheels on the bus* or *The Music Man* (Okki-tokki-unga). This should be your warm-up song at the beginning of every session; stay with the favourite and only consider changing every term or so if you really need to. The warm-up song both lets the children know that music is about to begin, makes them feel secure with its familiarity, and immediately gives them an action to do to get going.

You then need a greeting song to include and welcome all your children into music time. Make sure you include the names of any visiting siblings, toddlers or babies. You should greet each child with a name, a look and a smile, perhaps a wave too. Ideally, you should encourage the children to look at you as you sing, and respond with a smile or a wave. You should also encourage every single adult to join in the singing of this greeting song and you will find the older children join in too. Never expect all the children to join in singing all the songs. Both singing and doing actions at the same time are difficult for pre-school children, but are much more likely if the adults are doing it too. You will find activities suitable for warm-ups and greetings in Chapter 4.

Next move on to a couple of action rhymes. You will find ideas for these in Chapter 5 and many more in the books listed on the resources page at the end of this book. Keep the actions simple, starting with only one or two verses and building up until the children are familiar with the songs. Always try to have one well-known action rhyme and only introduce one new one in any one session. Make sure all the adults model the actions, especially if you yourself are reading unfamiliar words or playing an accompaniment. Some of the younger or less mature children might be helped by a hand-over-hand prompt. Take the songs slowly to give the children time to respond.

Now turn to Chapter 6 for ideas for looking and listening games. Take the chance throughout all the activities to praise good looking and listening, naming the children who are succeeding and trying to name all of them at some point.

Movement activities are included in Chapter 7. This has been placed near the end of the session since, once mobile, the children's initial attention and concentration might be lessened. Think ahead about the space you might need for this activity, and choose activities accordingly.

While you come back to the circle and rest from your movement, a spoken rhyme will provide a useful remission. Choose activities from Chapter 8. Finally (and sooner if you find attention waning; you will find you can stretch the music session to half an hour once you become more confident and fluent) choose activities from the 'band time' Chapter 9. Bring in the box of musical instruments which should have been hidden out of sight for the first part of the session. Allow the children to choose their own instruments, allowing non-ambulant children time to crawl, bottom-shuffle or be lifted to the box in order to take part in the choosing. I usually start with the simple activity 9.1, and then include two or three other band time activities, finishing with the grand march in activity 9.8.

Always finish with the same 'goodbye' song, again naming each child and encouraging a look, a smile or a wave. You will find suggestions for this also in Chapter 4.

Holding their attention – balance and flow

The pattern of the sessions has been designed to vary the pace and flow between action, song, looking and listening, speech, movement and instrument play. The children might quickly lose interest if you sat and sang songs for a full half hour. By varying the presentation in this way, you will find you can hold attention for 15 minutes or so when you first get going, gradually building up to 30 minutes. Do not attempt longer at this age and stage.

Use your own movements (approaching the children close, or moving between them) to hold eyes and attention. Keep one or two surprises up your sleeve to renew interest. Use 'props' to look at and to hold in order to catch their interest. Use their names and your praise to hold attention. Keep children with a short attention span next to an adult who can help to focus their watching and demonstrate what to do to them directly. Try to keep this fun and non-confrontational. Make the children *want* to join in rather than tell them they ought to.

Purchasing or making your own instruments – what to collect

You will need a range of instruments which make a sound when shaken, when beaten or when scratched. Avoid blowing instruments which will need disinfecting each time they are used, unless the children bring their own. Your percussion instruments can be either untuned or tuned (xylophones or chime bars); I prefer the former since the sound matches any other sound and you do not hear clashes of harmony. However, if you use only the black notes of a xylophone or chime bars in CDFGA then you have what is known as a 'pentatonic' scale and you will find that these sounds mixed together always sound pleasing. Make sure you have enough instruments for all the children and adults in the group. If you have a particularly popular instrument (usually the biggest drum) try to save up for more than one or help the children take turns fairly. I usually break band time at least once to suggest to the children that they might like to choose a new instrument.

On page 11 a possible shopping list is provided to help you choose a set of percussion instruments. How many you buy will depend on the size of the group, but try to get a good range. You can opt for colourful plastic instruments or you can buy 'real' instruments which can have a better sound though are not so easily sucked, dropped or banged. Make sure your collection represents a wide range of ethnicity and interest.

If you decide to make your instruments, make sure beans and pulses are securely contained. Remember that some uncooked beans are poisonous and be wary of younger children swallowing loose small parts or ingredients. You can make a range of sounds with dry pasta, rice, beans, sand, broken shell and gravel. You can make drums with saucepan lids or metal bowls with wooden spoons and make use of large used coffee tins which you can cover with bright paper or plastic. You will find further ideas for suppliers in the resources listed at the back.

Instrument	Have	To buy
Drums to beat with sticks e.g. snare drums		
Drums to beat with hands e.g. bongos		
Tambourines		
Jingle bells in rings and jingle bells on sticks		
Triangles – attach the beaters permanently with string		
Castanets		
Cabassa		
Guiro		
Wood blocks and beaters		
Indian bells		
Maracas		
Cymbals (to be used with careful supervision in order to protect noses and eyes)		

Chapter 2

Meeting the Early Years
and
Foundation Stage frameworks

Meeting all the children's needs inclusively

Many of you will be working in a school or registered setting and be following the *Curriculum Guidance for the Foundation Stage* (QCA and DfEE 1999) or the new Early Years Foundation Stage (EYFS). Therefore, you will already be familiar with the planning and record-keeping required under the Early Learning Goals and Stepping Stones, including the preparation for inspection. If you are including children with SEN, then much of your planning for individual children should overlap with the planning of your curriculum, your short, medium and long-term plan of activities, and your individual assessment of each child within your group.Others of you may be working with children under three and you will still be able to use the Music Makers approach to select activities that suit all the children, including those with additional needs.

Through your planning you can ensure that (a) you have covered all aspects of the curriculum or framework, (b) you have allowed each child to join in all the activities, (c) you have involved all your staff and (d) that you have information to share with parents so that they can support the activities at home. Those of you in registered Foundation Stage settings need to keep evidence that your whole curriculum is balanced and that most children are likely to achieve the Early Learning Goals by the time they finish the Foundation Stage. These Early Learning Goals are listed on page 69 and given a reference number which is cross-referenced to the activity pages to help you with this planning.

You should aim to make all your activities inclusive for children with special educational needs; they have joined your group to be a part of it and should be following the same framework, albeit at a level appropriate to their ability. You will need to look carefully at the child's strengths, needs and interests when planning how to include them in each activity. Although you might use strategies suitable for younger children to help those who are less mature in their development, take care to use songs, instruments and resources suitable to their actual age. A child of four who is learning similar skills to a two-and-a-half year-old is likely to develop low self-esteem if always provided with much younger rhymes and activities.

How your music session can contribute towards your curriculum or framework

If you look at each of the activity pages in Chapters 4 to 9, you will see a list of the Early Learning Goals towards which that activity contributes. This will be useful evidence when showing how you are planning to cover all the outcomes and how you are striving to provide a balanced curriculum. The areas of personal, social and emotional development and creative development figure largely, but you will also see how music can be usefully adopted to teach learning goals from the areas of communication, language and literacy, mathematical development, knowledge and understanding of the world, and physical development. Each goal has been given a reference number ready for cross-referencing the musical activities to the goals they contribute towards. Those of you that follow the monthly activities in *Nursery Education* and other Scholastic publications will be already familiar with this kind of referencing.

If you work with under threes, you will find that each activity is cross-referenced, this time to the *Birth to Three* framework. This should help you plan activities that cover each aspect of development and this system will map easily onto the EYFS framework.

You can, of course, adapt the approach for older children and integrate the planning of your activities with the National Curriculum. The author has found that most of the activities adapt well for older children. They can also be extended for able children by allowing them a greater say in the session and encouraging them to 'lead' and initiate ideas as well as to join in and to follow.

Planning effectively

When your early years setting is subject to inspection you may choose to hold your music making session as usual. Whilst it is unlikely that every area of learning will be covered in one session, the inspector will be able to look at your curriculum plans and record-keeping and see how you are using your music sessions to cover all aspects and areas of learning. You should keep other useful evidence of your planning, including examples of the children's musical activities and any photographic or video recording too.

Your planning should also show that you have a range of activities that contribute to your curriculum. Some should be in small groups, some in larger, but you should also plan opportunities for children to play independently, depending on the particular activity. Each activity should relate to a particular learning outcome and to the numbers, ages and stages of the children involved. The activity chapters in this book follow this requirement and show how this can be done in practice. Your session planning sheets, showing which activities you have used, which special needs targets and which Early Learning Goals/Birth to three/EYFS aspects are contributed towards, will prove useful evidence of your planning and teaching at inspection time.

Chapter 3

Welcoming a child with additional needs to the group

In this chapter we look at how you can include young children with special or very individual educational needs into your regular music sessions and how to plan for their needs. Those of you working in schools or registered early years settings are also shown how to have regard to the *SEN Code of Practice*. A registered early years setting is one that is registered with the LEA to receive funding for three and four-year old placements. There is a statutory duty for these settings to have regard to the guidance in this Code which details how to identify and plan interventions for children who have SEN. If you work with under threes, you can still use the Music Makers approach to target any children with additional needs or disabilities within your group.

Gathering information

Before you begin to plan activities to meet any particular special needs you will need to know what skills the child who has special needs already has, and decide what your targets should be. This assessment and target setting will provide the information you need to plan an individual education programme for that child, along the guidelines of the *SEN Code of Practice*. This will be explained later.

The assessment sheet which we developed in the Music Makers project is shown on page 73. We used this assessment in three ways. Firstly, we gave a copy to the parents of the child with special needs, as a way of showing the curriculum of activities we would be following, but also asking them to let us know what the child could do at a particular time, and what skills the parents would realistically like their child to learn in music group over the following term. They were invited to enter one tick in the initial assessment column if the child could sometimes do that skill, and two ticks if they could do it reliably in many different situations. This enabled us to select those skills which were perhaps emerging for the child and build on those first for a successful start. In planning 'next steps' for each child, we selected the skill that was only a little more challenging than the skill before, teaching step by very small step. Sometimes we found it necessary to break the steps down even smaller than those on the assessment sheet when we were teaching.

We also used the assessment form to send to other professionals already working with the child. These included physiotherapists, speech and language therapists, pre-school teachers, teachers at specialist nurseries, psychologists and health visitors. This enabled the whole team of professionals working with the child to contribute to the assessment and planning for that child. Thirdly, we added our own observations of how the child responded during the first session or two.

When we had received the replies, we were able to combine these together into a planned programme of activities for that child, and to return a term later to assess progress. On this occasion, we used our own observations of how the child responded in the group, and kept parents and professionals involved with the results of our teaching.

In practice, you might like to use the assessment sheet simply as an observation schedule, working out what the child can do now (that needs no further teaching or encouragement) and what you would like to target next.

A model for assessment and record-keeping

You will see that the assessment sheet is broken down into certain areas which relate, more or less, to the sections on the session planning sheet on page 75. These skills correspond to developmental stages from approximately six months to four years and, though in no particular order, are roughly ranked from easiest skill to most challenging within any one activity area.

The *SEN Code of Practice*

Perhaps you have a child attending who you already know has special educational needs. You may have been approached by parents, health visitor, social worker, or pre-school teacher and asked whether you could provide a part-time place for the child. In this case, you will need to gather information about who is already involved and use parents very much as experts on their own child to plan your approaches.

It could also be that you are identifying a special need for the first time within the group. Perhaps, even after a settling-in time, you have a child who is very insecure within the group, a child who appears to be playing at a very immature level, a child who finds eye contact and social interaction particularly difficult, or a child whose behaviour does not respond to your usual methods and approaches. It will be helpful if you understand the phased model given in the *Special Educational Needs Code of Practice* (DfES, 2001).

If you feel that you will need to adapt your approaches significantly in order to meet the needs of an individual child whose progress, behaviour or emotional state concerns you (that is to say their needs are *additional* or *different* to the usual), then you will need to plan approaches via *Early Years Action*, keeping parents or carers closely in touch as you follow a phased approach for assessing what the child needs to learn next, planning how you are going to teach it, and who is going to be involved. About one fifth of all children might need individual approaches at some stage of their school lives.

Once a child is on *Early Years Action*, you will need to adapt your approaches within the group to cater for that child, negotiating your approaches with parents or carers and meeting at least termly to review progress. If the child seems to need additional support from within your setting, you will need to produce an individual education plan (IEP) for the child, targeting particular learning outcomes and planning who is going to teach them, and how. Once again, this needs to be shared and negotiated with parents. In a nursery or reception class attached to a larger school, there will be advice available from the school's special needs co-ordinator or 'SENCO'. All registered settings now have their own SENCOs and Area SENCOs as well.

Children who continue to experience special educational needs despite this intervention may need assessment and guidance from outside professionals. You will find it helpful to talk with the local health visitor, early years advisory teacher or educational psychologist for advice on referral. Sometimes, you might need general advice on approaches for managing challenging behaviour, or for encouraging a child with autistic difficulties to join into a group. These children receive their support via *Early Years Action Plus*. A very few children may go on to receive statutory assessment and perhaps a statement of SEN which involves support and sometimes additional resources from the local education authority (LEA). In your IEP you will need to record the nature of the child's difficulty, the action you will take, what help the parents will provide, your targets for the term, and when you will be holding a review meeting with the parents.

How to use the activities to plan approaches for meeting SEN

Once you have combined all your initial assessment forms from parents and other professionals, you will be able to select target skills to include in your education plan for that child. In Music Makers, this can be done by using the assessment sheet to carry out an observation of a child during the music session and then drawing up an IEP around new targets you have selected. You will find an example on the next page.

First look at skills which the child can do sometimes but not always. Then move on to the next most difficult skill. Look for opportunities for generalising each skill into the rest of the play session, using the ideas in the activity Chapters 4 – 9.

> **Individual Education Plan**
>
> **Name:** Holly Smith
> **Phase:** Early Years Action
> **Nature of difficulty:** Holly's development is still immature and is about a year behind her age, according to the health visitor.
>
> **Action**
>
> 1. Elaine will ask the health visitor for further information and find out if any other professionals are involved.
> 2. Vicky and Sue will observe Holly over two music sessions and complete the initial assessment form.
> 3. Select activities for a regular music group which encourage Holly to look and to listen in the group and to copy actions.
> 4. Follow these activities up in the rest of the session; Elaine will work alongside Holly for part of each day.
> 5. Find out about training; Sue will find out about possible 'Portage' training next summer.
>
> **Help from parents:** John and Carrie will also fill in the initial assessment form, and Carrie will come in for music so that she can extend the activities at home.
>
> **Targets for this term**
>
> 1. Holly will look and listen to the music leader during each activity.
> 2. Holly will join in the keywords in a familiar action song.
> 3. Holly will begin to imitate simple actions, such as clapping and waving.
> 4. Holly will begin to play more constructively with the toys and playthings.
>
> **Review meeting with parents:** July 18th after morning session. Invite health visitor.

Step-by-step teaching

For children with significant and long-term special educational needs, you might find that steps need to be broken down very finely in order for the child to learn and develop. Learning occurs best if accompanied by success, so it is vital to plan activities at just the right level for the child to feel successful. Your praise and encouragement will make all the difference to this.

Use of praise and encouragement

One of the advantages of the musical approach is that it brings with it its own motivation and enjoyment. When you are involving a child with special needs in your group, you will need to ensure that an adult sits alongside, models all the actions, prompts the child to respond (with physical help if necessary) and makes the whole process fun and enjoyable. Your smiles, your constant praise, your enthusiasm will all be key elements to success. You can pick out any of the children by name to praise certain behaviours: '*Jed's* looking', 'Mari, you're watching me *beautifully*', 'Peter, you *are* marching well today'. One of the advantages of using a circle is that you can scan all the faces quickly and provide instant recognition of effort and success through your flashes of expression.

In responding to your children, you need to be always 'on your toes', ready to change the activity flexibly, ready to vary the pace, ready to swoop into band time if they are losing interest. I used to tell the parents not to worry about their child's behaviour in the group – if they did not concentrate, it would be my fault for not keeping it interesting enough! That is both the challenge and the amazing effect of running a music group.

16

Partnership with parents

You are required to keep parents and carers closely in touch with all your planning and intervention for children with special needs. This partnership and ongoing communication will work best if you share the good news as well as the bad right from the start. You will find it difficult to establish trust between you if you adopt the following attitude: 'Let's wait and see; we don't want to worry the parents until we know that something is really wrong'. Instead, you need to be planning and monitoring the children's progress and challenges all of the time, so that your special needs assessment and record-keeping arise naturally out of what you are doing day to day.

Providing outreach support and a warm welcome

Once you are running your music group with confidence, why not invite other children and parents who would benefit? You could also provide a newsletter to keep all your parents in touch with your musical activities, with particular reference to follow-up activities at home. Why not open your doors to other early years or special needs colleagues in the locality (such as childminder networks) to show them one practical way of meeting special needs and of including all children flexibly in your activities?

Contacting other parents

You will need to approach this sensitively. Sadly, the very act of categorising children as having 'special needs' can segregate the needs of these children from those of the rest of the population in people's minds. Try to make sure that your sessions are available to all children, regardless of need.

Your health visitor might be a useful contact if you decide to provide outreach to other parents and carers. Ask her or him to help you make sure you have invited any children to the group who might benefit. Perhaps there are children who, by nature of their development, do not attend their local early years setting but attend a child development centre instead. Perhaps there are children who are living in temporary foster care who would benefit from joining the group for sessions with their foster carer. Perhaps there are children whose behaviour has been challenging outside the home, but who might find it easy to behave during a half-hour's highly motivating music group. In other words, do consider inviting children to join just the music session, even if they are not a member of your local group.

In the Music Makers project, we wrote to parents of all children attending the local child development centre who were two, three or four years old. We asked them firstly if their child already attended a local pre-school group and whether that group would appreciate training in the setting up of a developmental music group. This book covers the training they received. Secondly we asked them whether they would like to join their local pre-school just for the half hour of the music session. We then matched families up to local groups willing to include them and willing to train in the approach.

Parents of children with a disability were always invited to be with their child during the sessions, sharing the fun and supporting their learning. We learned not to ask parents of older or school-age children to attend as a matter of course, since some felt that the sessions were an opportunity for their child to learn how to join in fully without them being present. However, the invitation to choose was always made.

Many other parents chose to join us also, and it was helpful to have an adult-child ratio for the whole group of at least four children to one adult. In a 'behaviour group' which we ran in conjunction with the local health visitors, we were delighted to welcome fathers and mothers together, the working partner managing to arrange to be with us in order to share some of the enjoyment of seeing their child learn and behave in a group with other children.

Chapter 4

Enjoying music together

In this chapter, you will find eight activities to help children 'warm up' to music time, to greet the children individually, and to say 'goodbye' at the end of the session. They are designed to build children's confidence and to form part of a regular routine in which children can anticipate what is happening next.

Activity 4.1   Warming up

Skill: To 'warm up' and to join in at the beginning of a music session.
Target link: G1 G2 G3 G4 L1 L2 V1 V5 M1 M2 S1 S2 S3 A3 A5 A7
Early Learning Goal link: PSE 1b and 3b; CLL 1b, 1d and 4a; PD 1a; CD 3a and 4a
Birth to Three framework link: stc3, stc4, skc2, cl3

What to do
Arrange your space for music session (see Chapter 1). Call the children to sit down in a circle and start playing an accompaniment or background music as you help them settle in order to signal that it is music time and to hold their attention. As soon as they are gathered, sing a warm-up song. Always start with a firm favourite, though you might change this from term to term. This becomes an important cue for the child with anxiety or learning difficulties that the familiar routine of music session is about to begin.

Choose a song with much repetition and simple actions, e.g. *If you're happy and you know it* (you will find the tune in *Apusskidu* [Pavelko & Scott]).

> *If you're happy and you know it, clap your hands* (x 2)
> *If you're happy and you know it, then you really want to show it*
> *If you're happy and you know it, clap your hands.*

Repeat with the simple actions 'wave your arms', 'stamp your feet', 'shout I AM'.

Support
If a child has difficulties doing the actions, demonstrate them clearly and ask the carer to place their hands gently over the child's to prompt. Alternatively the carer can clap onto the child's hands, or wave at the child. Do not expect all children to manage the 'I AM' but be delighted if you get any vocalisation at all at this point. Sometimes a child with language or communication needs might use the action for, say, *The wheels on the bus* as a signal that he is looking forward to music – be ready to see this as a sign of communication and respond appropriately.

Extension
Develop your own favourite words and phrases for the least verse, e.g. *If you're happy and you know it shout CAULIFLOWER!*

Follow-up ideas
- Look in *Okki-tokki-unga* for other very familiar and simple action rhymes.
- *The wheels on the bus* is another firm favourite. Develop your own version of the verses with the children's suggestions.

Activity 4.2   Greeting song

Skill: To encourage the children to greet each other at the start of the group.
Target link: V1 V3 V5 V6 S6 U1 A1 A4 (waving 'hello')
Early Learning Goal link: PSE 1b, 3a and 3b; CLL 1b and 1d; CD 4a
Birth to Three framework link: stc1, stc2, stc3, stc4, skc1, hc1

What to do

After the warm-up song, move straight into a greeting song. The aim is to greet each child by name and encourage a look, a smile, a wave, or even a joining in from the very confident ones. Let the children choose how they are going to respond and do not expect them to sing or speak to you unless they feel ready to. This song is best sung unaccompanied so that you can move around the circle. Tell all the adults in the circle that they must sing too to keep you company!

Move around the circle so that you can look each child in the face at their level. If a child has poor visual attention, give a touch on the shoulder or leg to engage attention.

This song can be sung to the tune of *Peter Pointer, Peter Pointer, where are you?*

> *Joshua Carter, Joshua Carter, Where are you?*
> *Here I am, Here I am, How do you do?*

Put the child's own name into the first line. If you prefer to stick to first names, sing 'Hello Joshua, Hello Joshua' instead. If you have a very shy child who hides into a carer, sing 'There (s)he is, there (s)he is' so that (s)he is still included.

As the children become more familiar with this greeting, encourage them all to wave at the child being greeted. This will help them learn each other's names.

Support

Teach a simple sign for a greeting such as a thumbs up to accompany the song. Children who are non-verbal might be able to respond by signing.

Extension

Older children enjoy singing the last two lines back to you, but never force this.

Follow-up ideas

- Use the children's names regularly before you talk to them in order to give respect and gain attention.
- Make sure you pronounce children's names correctly each time.
- Include any visiting babies and toddlers in your greeting song.
- If they enjoy it, sing the greeting song for certain children (for example, some children with language or communication difficulties) as they come in.
- Use name labels if you are leading an unfamiliar group.

Activity 4.3 Old Macdonald's Makaton farm

Skill: To help the children warm up using Makaton signs.
Target link: G1 G2 G3 G4 L1 L2 V1 V5 M1 M2 S1 S2 S3 S4 A3 A5 A7
Early Learning Goal link: PSE 1b and 3b; CLL 1b, 1d and 4a; PD 1a; CD 3a and 4a
Birth to Three framework link: skc1, skc2, skc3, cl1, cl3, cl4

What to do
Adopt this as one of your warm-ups to show that we do not only communicate with words. It is especially helpful if you have a child with additional needs who is learning to use Makaton sign language in your group. Talk to parents or visiting speech and language therapist about the signs the child is using and ask them to demonstrate the signs used in this song. You might like to enquire from the therapist about possible Makaton courses in your area. Alternatively, introduce the signs as part of a topic on 'senses'. All the children will enjoy using action songs with the signs.

Sing *Old Macdonald had a farm* (traditional). Stop at the point where you need to think of an animal and invite suggestions. 'What does a *cow* say?' 'Can you remember the sign for *cow*?' For each verse, have just one animal and do not tax memories by building the animals up cumulatively at this stage.

Here are some examples of Makaton signs:
- cow – two fists on your brow, moving up in the shape of two horns;
- sheep – two fingers at the sides of your face moving outwards to draw a curly fleece;
- pig – a fist on your nose with a screwing movement;
- horse – two fingers astride one finger and trotting along;
- goat – pull your beard down;
- cat – preen your whiskers;
- dog – sit up and beg with two paws up (ask parents for an actual demonstration).

Support
Use a picture, a visual demonstration and then hand-over-hands to teach signing.

Extension
Ask the speech and language therapist about any Makaton or other signing videos or DVDs (QEd supply a pack called *Accelerating Babies' Communication* by Tania Allen including *Sign with your Baby* by Joseph Garcia).

Follow-up ideas
- Use signing as a regular part of your playing and communication for those children who need it. Makaton is not used to replace spoken language, but to encourage it and to make the child's communication clearer.
- Show the other children how to use the signs too.

Activity 4.4 The shaking game

Skill: To tune in to looking and listening at the beginning of a session, and to loosen up.
Target link: L1 V2 V6 M2 M3 M4 M5 U9 A1 A2
Early Learning Goal link: PSE 1c, 3b and 4b; CLL 1b; PD 1a and 1b
Birth to Three framework link: stc2, stc3, skc3, cl3

What to do
This is an excellent activity for encouraging the whole group to concentrate as one. You need a large tambourine. Tell the children that you are going to play some shaking music. When they hear it they are to shake all over; shake their arms, their toes, their bodies all over. When it stops, they should stop too. Are they listening? Are they looking? Move round the circle as you shake the tambourine loudly, encouraging them to shake. Then beat the tambourine once loudly, stopping absolutely still. Praise children by name for looking and listening. Scan faces so you can use a flash of recognition to show children you have noticed them. Repeat three or four times, encouraging laughter and giggles as you shake and scanning all the children's faces when you have stopped. Keep this fun and challenging. Pretend to put it away, but then let it shake just one last time. Praise all the children for looking and listening so well.

Support
Practise this activity one-to-one first, then generalise it to the group.

Extension
Use other percussion instruments to suggest different actions e.g. a 'rainmaker' (broken shells and sand in a cylinder); when the children hear the rain, can they put their umbrellas up? When the rain stops, can they put them down again?

Follow-up ideas
- Use this activity to introduce shaking percussion instruments at Band Time (Chapter 9).
- Build it into other shaking and wobbling games, such as the Jellyfish song (page 23) or *Jelly on a plate* (page 22).

Activity 4.5   Jelly on a plate

Skill: To lose inhibitions at the start of a session.
Target link: L1 V2 V6 A1 A2
Early Learning Goal link: PSE 1c, 3b and 4b;
CLL 1b and 5b; PD 1a and 1b
Birth to Three Framework link: skc1, skc4, cl1,
cl2, cl3

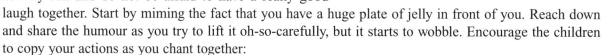

What to do
After a greeting song, move straight on to this chant.
Encourage children to wobble all over when they hear or
say the words 'jelly' and 'wibble wobble'. Make this
activity fun and do not be afraid to have a really good
laugh together. Start by miming the fact that you have a huge plate of jelly in front of you. Reach down
and share the humour as you try to lift it oh-so-carefully, but it starts to wobble. Encourage the children
to copy your actions as you chant together:

> *Jelly on a plate*
> *Jelly on a plate*
> *Wibble wobble, wibble wobble,*
> *Jelly on a plate!*

Now tell them to look behind them where they will find a large spoon. Mime finding yours and take a big
scoop out of your pretend jellies. What colour is yours? Chant together:

> *Jelly on the spoon* (etc.)

Finally, take a big mouthful and talk about the tastes and sensation, finishing with the verse:

> *Jelly in my tum!* (etc.)

Support
For children who find it hard to move independently, give a gentle shake or tickle.

Extension
Introduce role play and imaginary sequences into other action rhymes.

Follow-up ideas
- Follow up later in the session by making jelly!
- One group replaced their water tray with a jelly tray outdoors. Have plenty of bowls of warm soapy
  water available to mop up!

Activity 4.6   Jellyfish songs

Skill: To lose inhibitions at the start of a session.
Target link: L1 V2 V6 M2 M3 M4 M5 A1 A2
Early Learning Goal link: PSE 1c, 3b and 4b; CLL 1b and 5b; MD 1a; PD 1a and 1b
Birth to Three framework link: stc3, skc2, skc3, cl3

What to do
Start with the tambourine shake (page 21). Move on straight away to another wobbling song, this one can be sung to the tune of *Three blind mice*.

> *Three green jellyfish, three green jellyfish*
> *Sat upon a rock, sat upon a rock*
> *The first one felt like a swim, you know,*
> *And slithered away to the sea, you know,*
> *And left the rest on their own-i-o,*
> *Just two green jellyfish.*

Wobble all over for the 'jellyfish'. Raise your hands in the air and wobble them down all the way to the sea for the slithering. Repeat one more time until there is one jellyfish left on the rock. Older children might like to act this out as you sing. There is another version of this rhyme that can be chanted:

> *Three green jellyfish, three green jellyfish*
> *Three green jellyfish sat upon a rock!*
> *And one green jellyfish felt like a swim - so off he went:*
> *Wibble wobble, wibble wobble, wibble wobble, SPLOSH!*
> *DOWN into the sea!*
> *And there was only . . . left!*

Once again, use wobbling and hands to emphasise the actions and pause for the children to count between each verse.

Support
These rhymes work well for carers with young children on their knees.

Extension
Children can be encouraged and helped to make up their own simple number rhymes. At this stage, it does not matter if these do not rhyme and scan!

Follow-up ideas
Make jellyfish stick puppets with crepe or tissue paper and make them slither into the sea, one by one. This will make the counting a more concrete experience.

Activity 4.7   It's time to say 'Goodbye'

Skill: To give a look, a smile or a wave when told 'goodbye'.
Target link: V1 V3 V6 S6 U1 A1 A4
Early Learning Goal link: PSE 3a and 3b; CLL 1b, 1d and 4a
Birth to Three framework link: stc2, stc4, skc3, hc1

What to do
Use this song to close your session. Sing the 'Goodbye' song below, moving round the circle as you sing. Encourage all the other adults and any children who can to join in the song too. As you reach each child, look them in the face, smile and sing the song inserting their name. Encourage a look, a smile or a wave from each child. Some of the older or more confident children may well join in the 'Goodbye'. If a child is very shy and hides his/her head, give a light touch to show that you respect and value them as you sing 'goodbye'.

In case you do not read music, the note names are written down so that you can pick the tune out on a keyboard, piano or recorder. Leave gaps for the dashes. An apostrophe after the note name (D') means top D (the one nine notes above 'middle C'). Work the tune out first so that you can use it confidently during the session.

It's time to say   Good-bye   , It's time to say   Good-bye
D | B   B   A   A | G –   – D | B   B   A   A | G – –
Good-bye,   Good-bye,   It's time to say   Good- bye.
D' | B   –   – D' | B –   – D | B   B   A   A | G – –

Support
There are some children with communication difficulties who learn to sing 'goodbye' before they can speak it. You might wish to sing 'goodbye' at other appropriate times too.

Extension
Many groups make up their own versions of a goodbye song using the children's own ideas.

Follow-up ideas
Always get down to the child's level and greet or say 'goodbye' to the child with your full attention and respect. Do not automatically greet the adults first!

Activity 4.8   Moving on songs

Skill: To give a look, a smile or a wave when told 'goodbye'.
Target link: V1 V3 V6 S6 U1 A1 A4
Early Learning Goal link: PSE 3a and 3b; CLL 1b, 1d and 4a
Birth to Three framework link: stc1, stc2, stc3, stc4, skc1, cl1

What to do
These versions are useful if your music time does not fall at the end of your session and when the children are going to move on to another activity. At the end of music time, sing this song to each child as you encourage a look, a wave or a smile. You can dismiss each child from the circle as you all sing 'goodbye' to them. Have another helper or two on hand to encourage the children who are leaving the circle to move to the next activity, drinks time etc. The tune is the first two lines of *Twinkle twinkle little star*. Substitute the child's name in the second line.

> *Now it's time to say goodbye,*
> *Megan Jones, off you fly!*

Touch each child lightly to dismiss them, or shake hands as another variation (you need some sort of physical prompt to let them know when they can 'fly', or they will be up and off before they have looked at you and made their goodbyes).

Another version is to send the children off in pairs to start playing together. Name two children first and then sing this to the tune of *Girls and boys come out to play*:

> *Now is the end of music time*
> *If you want to go and play, that's fine!*

Support
For the partner version, pair any child with additional needs with a more confident child and take a moment to redirect them onto the next activity.

Extension
Some children might like to come with you on your journey around the circle and do the shaking hands or waving with you. Limit this to one at a time.

Follow-up ideas
- Make up other 'goodbye' songs, or make these up, as substitutes. Do not change too often in order to maintain familiarity.
- If you are enjoying music in a nursery or school setting, have your music time last thing. You can then use the first version as parents and carers arrive at the end of the session to collect their child.

Chapter 5

Songs and action rhymes

In this chapter, you are encouraged to make use of the wealth of activity songs and rhymes generally available. You will find the resource list on page 76 helpful. There are eight suggestions to start you off, but choose your action rhymes and songs flexibly and look out for new favourites all the time. Keep them simple and do not expect all the children to manage complicated series of actions. Help any children with physical difficulties make approximations of the action, gradually 'shaping' up to closer matches.

Activity 5.1   Jungle sounds

Skill: To join in a simple series of actions, including a one-two stepping rhythm.
Target link: G2 G4 V5 V6 M1 M2 M3 M4 M5 M6 S1 A2 A7
Early Learning Goal link: PSE 1b, 3b and 2a; CLL 2a and 4a;
PD 1a, 1b and 2a; CD 3a
Birth to Three Framework link: stc3, skc3, cl1, cl2, hc2

What to do
Learn this rhyme together:
> *Down in the jungle there's a rumbling sound*
> *Something's on the move and it's looking all around.*
> *Keep very still*
> *and listen if you will*
> *Hide yourself behind a tree and then you won't be found!*
> Hannah Mortimer

Use your tone of voice and gesture to create the right atmosphere of quiet listening and anticipation. When everyone is looking and listening, make a tiny sound. It might be a hiss of a snake or a chatter of a little monkey. Ask the children who they think is in the jungle. Repeat the rhyme as different children take turns to make a jungle sound. Prompt individual children with (whispered) ideas if they need them.

Now stand up as you move around the circle, tip-toeing for the first two lines, standing very still for the next two and crouching down to hide for the last.

Support
For children at an earlier stage of development, bounce them on a knee or lead them by the hands. Be aware of any timid children who might need additional reassurance.

Extension
Talk about animal sounds and habitats.

Follow-up ideas
- Look for other action rhymes with a simple one-two walking rhythm, such as 'One, two, buckle my shoe' (traditional).

Activity 5.2   Everybody copy me

Skill: To imitate a simple action.
Target link: G2 G3 G4 L6 V1 V5 V6 M3 M4 A1 A3
A4 A7
Early Learning Goal link: PSE 1a, 1b and 3b; CLL 1b, 1d
and 4a; PD 1b; CD 4a
Birth to Three Framework link: stc2, stc4, skc1, skc3, cl3

What to do
The tune is the same as for *Everybody do this* (by Mary
Miller) which you will find in *Okki-tokki-unga*. Tell the
children you are going to sing a copying song. Choose a very
simple action to start with like clapping hands, holding
arms up, touching noses, swinging legs. Sing the song and
model the action for children to copy.

> *Everybody copy, copy, copy,*
> *Everybody copy, copy . . .* (child's name)

You will find the older children singing as well as doing the actions, but the younger will just copy what
you are doing. After two or three goes, invite any child who wants to choose an action for you all to copy.
This activity is excellent for boosting self-esteem. Make sure you include children with restricted
movements or ideas so that you can give value to their choice and abilities.

If no-one volunteers, watch the children until someone does an action (such as swinging legs) and then
choose this for the next verse. That way, you are giving a child prestige even though he or she might have
been too shy to volunteer.

Support
Some children who might find this difficult will need an adult to encourage them to prompt an
approximate version of the action, hand-over-hand if need be.

Spend individual time with a child who has difficulties in copying, teaching them how to imitate. Keep
your movements large and exaggerated so that it is very clear what the child needs to copy. Use mirror
play to reinforce this. Prompt the child to do the actions if you need to, praising warmly for co-operation
or success.

Extension
Have a 'follow-my-leader' march around the room, taking it in turns to be the leader and set the style of
march or action for everyone else to copy.

Follow-up ideas
There is another version (to the tune of *Polly put the kettle on*):

> *Let's all do what (child's name) does*
> *Let's all do what (child's name) does*
> *Let's all do what (child's name) does*
> *It looks like this!*

Activity 5.3   Benjie hammers with one hammer

Skill: To imitate a simple action number rhyme.
Target link: G2 G3 L1 V1 V3 V5 V6 M1 M3 S8 U1 A1 A7
Early Learning Goal link: PSE 3b; CLL 1b and 1d; MD 1a, 2d and 3a;
PD 1a; CD 3a
Birth to Three Framework link: skc3, cl1, cl3

What to do
You will find a versions of this rhyme in *Okki-tokki-unga*.

> *Benjie hammers with one hammer, one hammer, one*
> *hammer*
> *Benjie hammers with one hammer, all day long.*
> *Benjie hammers with two hammers ...* (etc., up to
> five hammers).

> *Benjie's getting tired now* (slow right down)

> *Benjie goes to sleep now* (pretend to sleep)

> *Benjie's waking up now* (very fast with all hammers going!)

Here are the movements for the hammering verses

> Verse 1: hammer with one fist
> Verse 2: hammer with the other fist
> Verse 3: swing or hammer with one leg
> Verse 4: swing or hammer with the other leg
> Verse 5: shake or nod the head

As you all go to sleep, encourage the children to 'lie *down*' (or to put heads down and snuggle in if they are on a parent's knee). Leave a moment or two of silence to encourage quietness, listening and anticipation. Then sing the last waking-up verse briskly as you all 'hammer all over again!'

Support
Children with physical difficulties will need help and prompting to beat with one or two hammers. Instead of expecting them to hammer with fists, feet and head all at once (for five hammers), just concentrate on one movement or limb. Thus, once again, you have an activity which includes all your children but at different levels of ability involvement.

Extension
Use claves, beaters and percussion instruments to make the sound of hammers striking.

Follow-up idea
• Teach the children *Nick-nack-paddywack, give your dog a bone* (traditional).

Activity 5.4   Row, row, row your boat

Skill: To work with a partner, imitating a rocking action.
Target link: G3 L6 V3 M1 M3 A1 A2
Early Learning Goal link: PSE 3a, 3b and 6a; CLL 4a;
PD 1b
Birth to Three Framework link: stc4, skc1, cl3, hc2

What to do
You will be familiar with this traditional rhyme. If you
need to, ask a colleague or a parent for the tune.

> *Row, row, row your boat, gently down the stream,*
> *Merrily, merrily, merrily, merrily, life is but a dream.*

The first time you sing this, allow the children to rock in their places as if they are rowing a boat. Children on knees can be rocked gently, preferably facing towards parents. When the children are more familiar with the song, encourage them to join in pairs, facing each other and rocking gently forwards and backwards as they hold hands. Alternatively, younger children can be sat astride a knee with a grown-up as partner. Always aim for helping children join in fully with another child if at all possible.

Another variation for this song has as its second verse:
> *Row, row, row your boat, gently down the stream,*
> *If you see a crocodile, don't forget to scream!* (everybody screams!)

Families in our groups made up these further verses:
> *Row, row, row your boat, gently down the stream,*
> *If you see a tall giraffe, don't forget to laugh!* (everybody laughs!)

> *Row, row, row your boat, gently down the stream,*
> *If you see a hippopotamus, don't forget to make a lot of fuss!* (everybody cries!)

Repeat the first verse again to finish.

Support
Children with additional needs can be helped by a grown-up sitting behind them, legs either side on the floor.

Extension
It is your turn to make up more verses!

Follow-up ideas
- Try back-to-back rocking.
- Place all the children in a long line, sitting on the floor with legs each side of the child in front. Now row your long boat together.

Activity 5.5   Incy Wincy Spider

Skill: To look and copy a simple series of actions.
Target link: V5 V6 S6 A1 A2 A6 A7
Early Learning Goal link: CLL 1b, 1d and 4a; KUW 5b; PD 1b
Birth to Three Framework link: stc3, skc2, skc3

What to do
This is just one example of how you can use rhymes and chants to encourage actions. Once again, try to choose activities that allow *everyone* to join in within their own capabilities. In this rhyme, for example, some children will be able to copy a quite complicated finger to thumb 'climbing' movement as Incy climbs up the spout. Other children will, more simply, raise their arms in the air and wiggle fingers.

> *Incy Wincy Spider climbed up the water spout,*
> *Down came the rain and washed poor Incy out.*
> *Out came the sunshine and dried up all the rain,*
> *So Incy Wincy Spider climbed up the spout again.*
> (traditional)

Make your fingers climb upwards in the first line. Then let them fall with a sprinkling movement for the rain, washing Incy away. Let your hands lift again to trace the shape of the sun and move upwards as the rain dries. Then climb your fingers upwards again for the final line.

You may have come across other versions for this traditional rhyme – such as the version in which Incy climbed up the trees when the snow came down (and made poor Incy freeze). Fortunately the sun came out, melted all the snow so that he could have another go!

Support
For children at a much earlier stage in their development, their grown-up can use their own fingers to climb up the child.

Extension
Talk about spiders and explain why they are sometimes called our 'friends' (for catching flies).

Follow-up ideas
- Make dangly spiders to jiggle during this song.
- Link to the rainmaker game (bottom of page 21).

Activity 5.6   The Grand Old Duke of York

Skill: To learn the actions for 'up' and 'down'.
Target link: G3 G4 V5 V6 M3 U4 A7
Early Learning Goal link: PSE 3b; CLL 1b and 4a; MD 3c;
KUW 1c; PD 1b; CD 3a and 4a
Birth to Three Framework link: skc1, skc3, cll

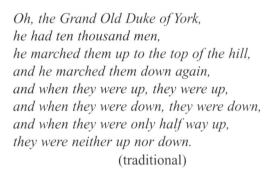

What to do
See whether you can find someone to accompany you on an
instrument to make this song go with a strong rhythm, otherwise,
have a grown-up beat a drum or a tambourine as you sing.
Encourage the children to raise their arms up in the air as the
Duke of York marches up the hill, and down to the ground as
he marches down again.

> *Oh, the Grand Old Duke of York,*
> *he had ten thousand men,*
> *he marched them up to the top of the hill,*
> *and he marched them down again,*
> *and when they were up, they were up,*
> *and when they were down, they were down,*
> *and when they were only half way up,*
> *they were neither up nor down.*
> (traditional)

Encourage the children to march round the circle raising arms up and down as you lead them, still singing
the song.

Support
Look for ways of including non-ambulant children too, perhaps in their walking frames or by everyone
singing it sitting down.

Extension
Alternatively, play your instruments loudly as you climb 'up' the hill, and softly as you come 'down'.

Follow-up ideas
• Use a variation of this at band time, bending low and reaching high as you march with the instruments
  (see Chapter 9).

There are further verses to this traditional rhyme:

> *They beat their drums to the top of the hill* (etc.)

> *They played their pipes to the top of the hill* (etc.)

Activity 5.7   Jack in the box

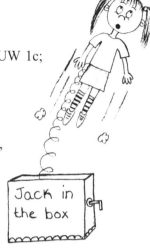

Skill: To listen out for a key word and then respond.
Target link: G3 G4 V5 V6 M3 S6 U4 A7
Early Learning Goal link: PSE 3b; CLL 1b and 4a; MD 3c; KUW 1c;
PD 1b; CD 3a and 4a
Birth to Three Framework link: skc3, cl1

What to do
Encourage all the children to make themselves as small as possible,
with their heads down low. When the song reaches the word 'up',
encourage everyone to sit up tall and follow the actions in the song.
Push children's heads down gently on the second last line, or
encourage them gently to push their own or a neighbour's. Wag your
finger at the children on the last line. The words fit approximately
to the tune *Girls and boys come out to play*.

> *Jack in the box jumps up in the air,*
> *he waves his arms and he waggles his hair,*
> *then I push him down again,*
> *saying 'Jack in the box, go back in your box!'*

Support
If you stay in a sitting position throughout this song, non-ambulant children can join in the same way as
the others. Laughing babies can be raised into the air.

Extension
Work out how to make a simple Jack-in-the-box, perhaps with a real child and a carton box!

Follow-up ideas
• Show the children a real Jack-in-the-box, but beware the rather startling cry that some models make.

Activity 5.8   The wheels on the bus

Skill: To join in a familiar action song.
Target link: G1 G3 G4 V1 V5 V6 M2 M3 M4 S2 S3
S5 A1 A3 A4 A7
Early Learning Goal link: PSE 3b; CLL 1d and 4a;
KUW 5b; PD 1b
Birth to Three Framework link: stc3, skc1, skc2, skc3, skc4,
cl1, cl3

What to do

You are sure to be familiar with this song, and it makes a very
good warm-up song too. The main thing is to choose actions
which everyone can do, whatever their ability. You may be
able to target particular actions that some of the children
with special needs are mastering at the time, such as
clapping hands or waving goodbye. Here are some ideas
for keeping the actions simple:

> *The children on the bus go wriggle, wriggle, wriggle . . .*
> *The mums on the bus go tickle, tickle, tickle . . .*
> *The people on the bus all wave goodbye . . .*
> *The babies on the bus all clap their hands . . .*

We usually accelerate the last verse as the driver goes 'brm brm brm' as we move our steering wheels
round the corners.

Support

Sometimes, children with speech and language difficulties might be practising certain sounds with their
speech and language therapist. These exercises might be built into a song like this, for example:

> *The birds in the trees go la la la . . .*
> *The babies on the bus go wa wa wa . . .*
> *The engine on the bus goes pu pu pu . . .*
> *The doors on the bus go hisssss . . .*

Extension

Encourage the children to think of their own verses. For example, one group always has a certain dog that
gets on the bus and causes trouble for everyone!

Follow-up ideas

* Sing *The children in playgroup go . . .* (etc.)

* Arrange chairs in the centre for some of the children to sit on the bus.

* Adapt the song for a train journey.

Chapter 6

Looking and listening games

In this chapter, there are eight tried and tested activities that encourage children to look, listen and to attend in a group situation. Music tends to be particularly motivating and enjoyable and so it makes it easier for children to attend, to join in and behave appropriately in the group, whatever their age and stage.

Activity 6.1　Find the sound

Skill: To turn towards a sound.
Target link: L1 L5 V2 V4 U9
Early Learning Goal link: PSE 1c; CLL 1b; PD 2a; CD 2a
Birth to Three Framework link: skc3, cl1

What to do
Choose an adult to help you. One of you pick up a tambourine and shake it so that the children can *see and hear* it. Tell them what it is called and pass it round the circle for everyone to have a go. The other adult should pick up the jingle bells and do likewise. Now stand outside the circle, one of you at each end.

Tell the children that you are going to hide your instrument behind your backs and take it in turns to shake it. Can the children guess where the sound is coming from?

Wink at your colleague so that (s)he plays the instrument, shaking it behind her/his back. Invite the children to 'find' the sound. Wait until almost all eyes are turned to the correct place, then reveal the instrument and shake it again so that they can all see. Praise their looking and their listening. Have about two goes each, varying which of you plays.

Support

- The adult holding the instrument can call a child's name to focus attention.
- For younger children, there is the added clue of where everyone else is looking or pointing to add extra support.

Extension
Build up to four instruments at compass points of the circle.

Follow-up ideas

- One of you hide behind a screen or piece of furniture and make a sound with an instrument. Can a child (or child and carer together) select which instrument from a choice of three is making that sound?

Activity 6.2   The pointing game

Skill: To point towards a sound.
Target link: L1 L5 V2 V4 U9 I1 I2
Early Learning Goal link: PSE 1c; CLL 1b; PD 2a; CD 2a
Birth to Three Framework link: stc4, skc3

What to do

In this game you take it in turns to be in the
middle of the circle. It is best if you have the
first go so that the children can understand
what to do. Tie a loose scarf around your head,
or hold a pad to your face so that you cannot
see. Make sure another adult in the circle helps
the children. The children should choose an
instrument and pass it from person to person
around the circle, no-one making a sound with
it. You then wink at one of the children who
should make a sound with it. The child in the
centre must try to point to where the sound is
coming from. Continue for several turns then
let someone else take a turn in the centre.

Support

For younger children, this is best done as an activity to teach the words 'gently' and 'quietly' – the children
pass the instruments and the adult points.

Extension

Older children can cope with the pointing role. You might consider passing two instruments around the
circle at once to make this activity more challenging.

Follow-up ideas

- If a child is worried about covering their eyes, try offering them a woolly hat to pull down, or a soft
  toy to burrow into.

- Use a signal to make the instrument change directions from time to time.

- Ask for the same gentleness when the children return their instruments to the box at the end of music
  time. Pretend to close your eyes to see if you can hear the instruments landing!

Activity 6.3   Feely bag

Skill: To use touch and sound to identify a musical instrument.
Target link: L1 L5 V2 V4 U9 I1 I2
Early Learning Goal link: PSE 1c; CLL 1b; PD 2a; CD 2a and 4a
Birth to Three Framework link: skc3, cl1

What to do
Show the children three instruments, perhaps a tambourine, the bells and the castanets. Pass them each round the circle and let the children make a sound with them. Now tell the children that you are going to hide them all inside a bag. Choose a big drawstring bag that you can easily reach inside. Place all three instruments inside. Now reach in and play one of them. Then ask: 'Would anyone like to come and feel inside the bag for the right instrument?' Alternatively, invite a child to pull the instruments out, one at a time, and play them one after the other, asking: 'Was it that one?'

Support
For children who have difficulties in remembering, have two of each instrument and continue to play one whilst they feel inside the bag for one that is the same.

Extension
Older children might be able to identify the instrument just from its feel and sound.

Follow-up ideas
- Play 'sound lotto' games.
- Make your own tape of familiar musical instruments and invite the children to identify or match them to encourage links between listening and looking.

Activity 6.4 A listening walk

Skill: To listen to sounds and identify them in the environment.
Target link: L1 L5 V2 V4 U9
Early Learning Goal link: PSE 1c; CLL 1b and 1d; PD 2a; CD 2a and 3a
Birth to Three Framework link: stc4, skc3, skc4, cl1, cl2

What to do
Tell the children you are all going to leave the circle and go on a short listening walk. This can be indoors or outside. If indoors, you will need to think ahead of certain sounds the children will be able to identify (the cars outside, the drip of a tap, the bubbles of the fish tank, the singing of children in the hall, the tune of a radio, the clatter of the bricks, and so on). Lead them off and choose different places to stop. Invite the children to shut their eyes and then, after a moment, talk together about all that you can hear.

Support
Stay close to younger children. Point out the sounds and either draw their attention to what you can hear together or offer choices – 'Listen! Was that a fire engine or an elephant?!'

Extension
Make your own tape recording of familiar household sounds (a lavatory flushing, a kettle boiling, a vacuum cleaner, a washing machine, a telephone ringing, a doorbell, etc.) and see if the children can identify them. You could also match these to pictures or to real items. See page 76 for further resource suggestions.

Follow-up ideas
- Use the instruments to provide sound effects for a short story.
- From time to time, have a quiet moment in circle time to listen for any sounds.

Activity 6.5   The dinosaur hunt

Skills: To listen to and repeat short phrases; to remember a sequence of actions.
Target link: G2 G4 V6 A2 A3 A7
Early Learning Goal link: PSE 1a, 2a and 3b; CLL 1d; PD1a and 1b
Birth to Three Framework link: skc3, skc4, cl1, cl2

What to do
Wait until the children are really confident. Most of them love this activity (it is a version of *We're Going on a Bear Hunt* by Rosen & Oxenbury). Hide a plastic dinosaur somewhere in the room so that you can 'find' it at the end of the dinosaur hunt.

Tell the children what you are going to do. Everything you say, they are to repeat. Make sure you have plenty of adults to help the children copy you.

> *We're going on a dinosaur hunt* (they repeat as you all march round)
> *I'm not scared* (they repeat as you all point to yourselves proudly)
> *Beautiful day* (they repeat as you all point up to the clear sky)
> *Oh oh . . .* (they repeat as you all stop still)
> **Grass** (they repeat)
> **Tall, wavy grass** (they repeat as you all make a swishing hand movement)
> *You can't go over it* (they repeat as you all make a gesture or sound for 'over')
> *You can't go under it* (they repeat as you all gesture 'under')
> *Got to go through it* (they repeat, all make huge steps, saying 'swish swish swish')

Verse 2: (For bold italics) **mud, dark squelchy mud** – make squelchy Wellington-boot steps.
Verse 3: **nettles, tall stingy nettles** – jump over them going 'ow! ow! ow!'
Verse 4: **a cave, a dark echoey cave** – feel your way in making echo noises.
Verse 5: **a dinosaur! Let's run home!** – reverse all the sounds as you run back to base. First make echoey noises, then nettles, then mud, tall wavy grass, and then arrive safely home and celebrate.

Support
Make sure that all the children and older babies have a chance to join in, regardless of mobility.

Extension
Invite the children to help you make up new verses.

Follow-up idea
• Use art and craft activities to create a picture story or frieze all about the dinosaur adventure. Use this to help the children sequence their ideas.

Activity 6.6   Hunt the mouse

Skill: To discriminate between loud and soft sound.
Target link: L1 L7 V5 U6
Early Learning Goal link: PSE 1c; CLL 1b; CD 2a and 4a
Birth to Three Framework link: skc3, skc4, cll

What to do
This is a variation of the traditional party game 'Hunt the thimble'. Invite one child to have the first go. Have one adult lead the child away just while you hide the toy mouse (or whatever you decide to hunt). Sit the children in a circle and give the toy to one child to hide within their clothing. Make sure all the children except the seeker have seen where it is hidden, focusing the attention of any children who have difficulty in noticing things. Remind impulsive children not to give away the secret!

Now invite your seeker back into the room. Tell him/her that one of the children is hiding the toy. Let another adult lead him/her around the inside of the circle whilst the rest of you sing loudly:

   How warm you are, how warm you are, how warm you are, how warm
   (to the tune of *Auld Lang's Syne*)

or:

   How cold you are . . . (sung softly, depending on whether the seeker is close to, or far away from, the toy).

You should be able to make it very obvious from your exaggerated response when the seeker is standing in front of the correct child. Invite him/her to tap the shoulder and the child tapped should reveal whether or not they are hiding the toy. This can generate tremendous giggling!

Support
Carry or lead smaller children by the hand.

Extension
Play 'hunt the thimble' (or similar) around the room, using progressively smaller objects which have to be looked for carefully.

Follow-up ideas
• Repeat the louds and softs with musical instruments instead of singing.

Activity 6.7   Honey bear

Skill: To locate a sound.
Target link: L1 L7 V5 U6
Early Learning Goal link: PSE
1c; CLL 1b; CD 2a and 4a
Birth to Three Framework
link: stc4, skc3, cl1

What to do
You need a set of jingle bells.
Show these to the children and tell them that they are Mrs (or Mr) Bear's honey pot! Invite an older, more confident child to come into the centre of the circle and sit down next to the bells. Chant together:

> *Isn't it funny how a bear likes honey!*
> *Buzz, buzz buzz, I wonder why she does?*
>   (adapted from A. A. Milne)

> *Go to sleep, Mrs Bear!*
> *Don't you peep Mrs Bear!*
> *Or someone might take your honey!*

At this point, encourage Mrs Bear to curl up and go to sleep. Wink or point to one of the children who should tiptoe up and take the bells as quietly as possible and return to sit down in the circle. Ask all the children to put their hands behind their backs, including the child with the bells. Call:

> *Wake up Mrs Honey Bear!*
> *Someone has taken your honey!*

Ask all the children to shake their hands, still hidden behind their backs. Help Mrs Honey Bear move around the circle until she thinks she knows which child is shaking the bells. She should touch that child's knee who should then hold up hands, with or without the instrument. This continues until the honey is found and these two children swap places.

Support
Younger children can work with a grown up partner or parent.

Extension
Children will play this 'till the cows come home'! Challenge them to remember whose turn it is next time you play.

Follow-up ideas
• This is a quiet version of the traditional (we think) party game in which Mrs Honey Bear and the 'thief' race around the outside of the circle with the last one back becoming Mrs Honey Bear next. Our groups found this rather too wild, but it might suit an older children's party.

Activity 6.8   Pass the sound

Skill: To practise handling objects carefully and gently and to locate sounds.
Target link: L1 L7 V2 V6 U6 I1 I10
Early Learning Goal link: PSE 3b; PD 2a and 4a; CD 2a and 4a
Birth to Three Framework link: stc4, skc3

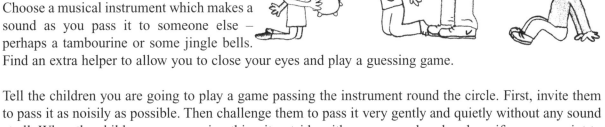

What to do
Choose a musical instrument which makes a sound as you pass it to someone else – perhaps a tambourine or some jingle bells.
Find an extra helper to allow you to close your eyes and play a guessing game.

Tell the children you are going to play a game passing the instrument round the circle. First, invite them to pass it as noisily as possible. Then challenge them to pass it very gently and quietly without any sound at all. When the children are managing this, sit outside with your eyes closed and see if you can point to where you think the instrument has got to. Praise them constantly for being so quiet and gentle.

Support
Place your helper next to the younger children to help and encourage them.

Extension
Allow your older children to take a turn guessing.

Follow-up ideas
* Practise playing instruments loudly and quietly.
* Practise singing loudly and quietly.
* Follow up with these words in the rest of the session; challenge children to close a door quietly or walk past another room quietly?

Chapter 7

Movement and rhythm games

Here you will find eight activities that encourage children to enjoy movement and listen to rhythm and beat. If you are including children with physical and mobility needs, you may find that they feel less inhibited and challenged when moving to a musical activity. Wait until your group has settled down (after two or three sessions) before introducing movement otherwise you might find it hard to settle the children again afterwards.

Activity 7.1   Drum Beats

Skill: To copy the rhythm of your name.
Target link: G3 L6 V3 V6 U1 A1 I3 I6
Early Learning Goal link: CLL 3a and 3b; PD 5a; CD 4a
Birth to Three Framework link: stc1, stc2, stc4, skc3, skc4, cl4

What to do
This activity makes a good greeting activity too. You will need a large drum – a large tambour or bodhran is excellent, but other drums or plastic containers can be used too. Invite the children to beat their first names on the drum.

Show them what you mean. Say: 'Hello Phil-ip', 'Hello Car-ol-ine', 'Hello Ah-hyun', beating the syllables of the names as you say them. Now move around the circle, giving the beater to each child, and saying 'Hello . . . ', encouraging them to beat their names to you.

The joy of this activity is that you should be able to guarantee total success, regardless of level of ability. Some children will manage this activity all by themselves and even be able to tackle their full names with practice. Others will need you to whisk the drum away after the correct number of beats and therefore succeed with your help.

Support
For children who find it hard to hold a beater, a hand or fist could be used instead, perhaps with a physical prompt (hand-over-hand) from the parent or helper.

Extension
Older children can try to beat the syllables of their full names.

Follow-up ideas
- Always have a strong drum beat from one of the adults at marching and band time.
- Have sufficient drums for everyone to feel they get a regular 'go' at band time as they tend to be the most popular instrument. Make sure the quieter and shyer children have a chance to make a lot of noise too.
- Place a selection of drums in the centre and chant:
  Drums, drums, beat the drums
  If you (. . .), you can beat the drums' (add a simple instruction such as 'if you are wearing blue' or 'if you came on the bus'. Only those children should come into the circle and beat the drums until it is time for the next go).

Activity 7.2   Cobbler, Cobbler

Skill: To move to a simple one–two rhythm.
Target link: G3 G4 L6 M1 M3 M4 M5 A1
Early Learning Goal link: CLL 1b, 3b and 4a; PD 1a;
CD 4a
Birth to Three Framework link: skc1, skc3, hc2

What to do
You will need a visual prop here. Try to get hold of some big work boots or heavy shoes. Encourage all the children to kneel down in a circle with both hands on the floor. Put your two hands in your heavy boots and raise them up and down to stamp a strong one–two rhythm. Can the children make the same rhythm? (If you have the time, they could all take shoes off and put them on their hands, kneeling). Chant this traditional rhyme as you 'walk' your hands.

> *Cobbler, cobbler, mend my shoe,*
> *get it done by half past two.*

or

> *Down at the bottom of the deep blue sea,*
> *catching fishes for my tea,*
> *how many fishes can you see?*
> *one . . . two . . . three . . .*

Support
Children at a younger stage of physical development might enjoy having arms or legs swung to the beat, or bouncing when held in a standing position.

Extension
Try a four-time rhythm with a 'one, two, three' (rest) to the chant of *Hot Cross Buns.*

Follow-up ideas
*   Look for other rhymes or songs with a steady marching rhythm, e.g. *The Grand Old Duke of York* (page 31), *Nick-nack-paddywack* (to a slow rhythm) etc.
*   Choose some tunes with a strong one–two rhythm at marching time. Use a loud drum to keep the beat, or stamp with your booted feet as you lead the march.

 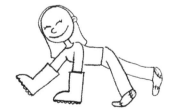 

Activity 7.3   Musical bumps and old favourites

Skill: To start and stop moving to music.
Target link: G2 L3 L4 V5 M2 M6 U5
Early Learning Goal link: PSE 1b; CLL 1b; PD 1a and 1b; CD 3a
Birth to Three Framework link: stc4, skc3, hc2

What to do
These activities are almost too obvious to include, but they are old favourites for the children and do encourage independent movement, looking and listening. Your task is to think of all your children, regardless of need, and plan how you can include them within their own abilities.

- Musical bumps – play a musical tape and encourage the children to flop to the floor when the music stops.

- Musical statues – encourage the children to keep still when the music stops.

- Musical partners – encourage the children to hold hands with a partner when the music stops (make sure there is an even number of children).

- Musical hats – encourage the children to put on a hat when the music stops (have enough for everyone and spread them out over your floor area).

- Musical instruments – encourage the children to choose a musical instrument when the music stops and play the tape for a short passage whilst they play them.

These versions are not competitive, and no-one is 'out'. However, you should be able to involve all the children and also find some good mixing together of all the children in the process.

Support
Pair younger children with a helper.

Extension
Set challenges for musical statues, for example: 'When the music stops make a spiky/scary/floppy (etc.) shape'.

Follow-up ideas
There are other musical party games could be adapted to encourage movement, looking and listening:
- Pass the teddy (instead of parcel),
- *The Farmer's in his den*,
- *Ring-o-ring-o-roses* (which can be played in a sitting position if some of the children are non-ambulant, dropping your arms to the floor for 'all fall down'; this can also lead into the one-two rhythm you have been practising on page 43.

Activity 7.4   The kangaroo song

Skill: To bounce to the rhythm of a beat, and have fun in movement.
Target link: G2 L6 V5 M1 M5
Early Learning Goal link: PSE 1b; CLL 4a; PD 1a; CD 3a
Birth to Three Framework link: stc3, skc3, hc2

What to do
This is a very enjoyable activity which children can join in, in a variety of ways. Older and physically able children can bounce to the beat. Other children and older babies can bounce in a standing position whilst being supported, or can be bounced on a knee.

Any bouncy music will do, though you will find the *Kangaroo song* in *Apusskidu* (Pavelko and Scott) particularly useful. The children should sit still for the verse, but can bounce in the air for the chorus. Repeat the song two or three times.

Here is a chant that would also work or you can easily make up your own:

Bouncy, bouncy kangaroo
I can bounce as high as you!
Bouncy bouncy – you bounce too
Bouncy bouncy kangaroo!

If you feel that the children are getting very excited, try this with a smaller group, or see if they can sit on the floor and pretend their hands are the kangaroos.

Support
Encourage younger children to face their carers or helpers whilst they are gently bounced on a knee.

Extension
Help older children make up their own bouncing chant.

Follow-up ideas
- Look for pieces of music with a bouncy, light beat to move to.
- Look up songs about Noah's Ark or zoos to follow the animal theme, for example, *The animals went in two by two* (traditional) or *Daddy's taking us to the zoo tomorrow* (Paxton) both in *Apusskidu*.

Activity 7.5   Five little speckled frogs

Skill: to make a movement to a key word.
Target link: G3 M1 M5 S8 U8 A2
Early Learning Goal link: CLL 1b and 4a; MD 1c and 2a; KUW 5b; PD 1b; CD 4a
Birth to Three Framework link: skc1, skc2, skc3, skc4, cl1, hc2

What to do
Look for the well-known song *Five little frogs* from *Apusskidu*. Ask children to volunteer to be one of the five frogs who should all crouch in the middle of the circle. You will find that you need to crouch there too to lead the actions.

When you reach the word 'jumped', then all the frogs should jump from a crouching position into the air and one should jump out of the 'pond' back into the circle. Pause the song at the end of each verse to count on your fingers how many frogs are left. Encourage the children to hold out their fingers to count, with an adult sitting close to prompt children who need help. This activity is great fun when done with props (see resources section).

Support
- For children with mobility problems, invite them to make their hands into the jumping frogs or give them bean bags to toss upwards at the key words.
- For children with short attention spans, start at three and work downwards.

Extension
Make a pond of stretchy green/blue Lycra and encourage the children to hold the edges as you toss bean bag frogs in, one verse at a time.

Follow-up ideas
- Look for songs that require actions to certain key words, for example, 'All fall *down*'. Encourage those children who have limited understanding to anticipate the actions, or to join in with the key word.
- Chant '*Five* fat sausages sizzling in the pan, all of a sudden one went *bang*!', clapping on the bang and, again, counting fingers between verses. When you get to '*No* fat sausages sizzling in the pan', chant this verse in a whisper and finish with 'But all of a sudden the pan went ***bang***!'

Activity 7.6   Heads, shoulders, knees and toes

Skill: To point to different body points.
Target link: G3 V5 V6 M3 U2 A1
Early Learning Goal link: PSE 3b; CLL 1b; KUW 1b;
PD 1a and 1b; CD 4a
Birth to Three Framework link: stc1, stc3, skc2, skc3, cl1

What to do
This activity is included to show how a very familiar rhyme or song can be adapted to include all children regardless of need. This is a well-known traditional tune:

> *Heads, shoulders, knees and toes, knees and toes,*
> *Heads, shoulders, knees and toes, knees and toes,*
> *Eyes and ears, and mouth and nose,*
> *Heads, shoulders, knees and toes, knees and toes.*

Start very slowly and allow most of the children to join in independently from the start, copying your actions as you point to each body part on yourself. Pair each child who is still learning body parts with a helper or parent.

The first time through, the helper should point to each part mentioned on the child, emphasising the key word: 'Head . . . shoulder . . . knee . . . toes . . . eye . . . ear . . . mouth . . . nose . . .'

The second time through, take it just as slowly, but ask the helpers to encourage (hand-over-hand if necessary) the children to point to themselves.

The third time through, take it at a tremendous rate for fun. The helpers should do the pointing again onto their child, ending with a laugh and a tickle. Meanwhile the children who are joining in the activity independently will have the challenge of doing so very quickly.

Support
This activity can be enjoyed passively by even the youngest babies – simply sing as you gently touch.

Extension
There is a version for older children in which you progressively miss out more and more body parts each verse as the children continue to point correctly.

Follow-up ideas
- Look in Chapter 8 for more activities that help the teaching of body parts.

- Build in body parts to the introduction song *If you're happy and you know it, touch your head* etc.

Activity 7.7   The crocodile song

Skill: To recognise body parts and to change positions.
Target link: G2 V1 U2 A7 M2 M3 M4
Early Learning Goal link: PSE 1b; CLL 1b and 4a;
KUW 5a; PD 1a
Birth to Three Framework link: stc4, skc3, cl2, hc2

What to do
This favourite activity has been included for older children – not for the faint-hearted, this one!

Gather in a circle. Start by standing, though look for ways of including children who cannot stand too (they will need a parent or helper to help them get into different positions). Hold hands and swing arms as you sing the chorus. The tune is the same as *In and out the dusty bluebells*.

> *I'm being eaten by a great big crocodile,*
> *I'm being eaten by a great big crocodile,*
> *I'm being eaten by a great big crocodile,*
> *I don't like it at all!*

Now say: 'Oh no! He's eaten my toe!' and get onto your knees. Repeat the chorus from your new position, inserting these verses after each chorus:

> *Oh my! He's got my thigh!* (lie on tummies but push up from the waist)
> *Oh lummy! He's got my tummy* (lie prone with head pushed up)
> *I think I'm dead! He's got my head!* (lie flat on your tummies)
> *Hurray we shout! He's spat me out!* (up you all get)
> (with acknowledgements to the Folk Camp Society where I first heard this, HM).

Support
This is a funny rhyme for children who enjoy being on their tummies. Continue to gently touch the body part being sung about.

Extension
This makes an enjoyable game for parties and cub/brownie groups, etc.

Follow-up ideas
*   Look for ways of adapting other traditional circle dances to include all the children, for example, *Here we go looby loo*; *Hokey Cokey*; *In and out the dusty bluebells*; *Wind the bobbin up*; *One two three four five six seven.*

Activity 7.8   Dinner on the train

Skill: To move faster and slower to a spoken rhythm.
Target link: G2 G4 V5 V6 M1 M2 M3 M4 M5 M6 M7 S1 A1
Early Learning Goal link: PSE 3b; CLL 2a, 3b and 4a;
PD 1a and 1b; CD 2a and 4a
Birth to Three Framework link: stc3, skc1, skc2, skc3, skc4, cl2

What to do
This is a good activity to insert just before marching time when you are already in a long line. Think ahead about how you are going to involve children with a range of needs. Children who are standing with support, but not yet walking, may like to bounce in a standing position and supported by a helper in the centre of the ring.

Tell the children that you are going on a pretend train journey. You are going to have your dinner on the train, but it's a very funny dinner because it's back to front! Can they copy what you do?

Chant these words to sound like a steam train gathering momentum. Churn your arms like the pistons on the wheels, and move faster as it goes.

> *Cof-fee, cof-fee,*
> *cof-fee, cof-fee,*
> *cheese and biscuits, cheese and biscuits,*
> *cheese and biscuits, cheese and biscuits,*
> *chocolate pudding, chocolate pudding,*
> *chocolate pudding, chocolate pudding,*
> *bangers and mash, bangers and mash,*
> *bangers and mash, bangers and mash,*
> *SOOOOOOOOOOOOOUP!*

Raise your fist in the air for this final whistle blow!

Support
If one of the children is learning how to blow, invite them to blow a whistle to start the train.

Extension
Make a chant together out of other words which have distinct rhythms. For example, look at titles in your book corner: *Peace at Last* (x4), *Topsy and Tim* (x4), *Very Hungry Caterpillar* (x4) *Spot!*

Follow-up ideas
- Start softly as well as slowly, building up speed and volume together.
- Sing other train songs, for example, *The wheels on the train go round and round.*

Chapter 8

Concepts and understanding

This chapter contains eight activities that encourage children's understanding of keywords and concepts. If you are including children with additional needs, you will find that those with learning and language difficulties may find it particularly hard to understand abstract concepts and these activities aim to link concept with action in a concrete way. All toddlers will benefit from rhymes and songs that show them what words actually mean by linking words and actions together.

Activity 8.1   Favourite colours

Skill: To look for and identify a named colour.
Target link: V5 V6 U7
Early Learning Goal link: PSE 1a; KUW 1c and 2a; CD 1a
Birth to Three Framework link: skc2, skc3, skc3, cll

What to do
Tell the children you are going to sing a song together all about colours. This song fits to the first four lines of the *Eton Boating Song*:

> *I have a favourite colour,*
> *My favourite colour is* **red***,*
> ***Red** is the colour that **Jonathan** wears,*
> *Everyone look for* **red***.*

When you reach the words in bold italics, add the name of one of the children who is wearing a lot of a particular colour.

Stop the song while you help all the children look for the colour red on their clothing. Show them the colour on your own clothing that matches. Point out children who are wearing similar clothes. Ask whose favourite colour red is. Repeat the song for a new colour and a new child. Encourage the children to join in once they know the song. Encourage them to help each other find the colours and make sure each child feels included.

Support
Help the younger children to look for the colours. They may find it easier to find a piece of clothing which matches a colour you show them, rather than to pick a colour out from its name alone. If the children wear a uniform, distribute coloured bands first.

Extension
Play a guessing game: 'I am thinking about someone who is wearing a red jumper and who has a baby sister here. Who is it?'

Follow-up ideas
- Introduce songs about rainbows.
- Comment on the colours in the children's clothes as you greet them: 'Hello, Prasarn, you are wearing a lot of red today. I think we ought to sing the colour song!'

Activity 8.2   Four currant buns

Skill: To join in a simple number rhyme.
Target link: S1 S6 S8 U8
Early Learning Goal link: CLL 4a;
MD 1b and 1c
Birth to Three Framework link: skc3, skc4,
cl1, cl2

What to do
You may know this traditional rhyme which you can
chant together.

> *Four currant buns in a baker's shop,*
> *Round and fat with sugar on the top,*
> *Along came* (child's name) *with a penny one day,*
> *Bought a currant bun and took it away.*

You can substitute a different child's name for each verse.

Pause between each verse to hold up and count fingers (or for a helper to touch and count fingers on a child who needs help), and repeat the verse until there are no buns left. You can also play this with real props of buns or card pictures. Choose someone to be the baker, give them the cardboard buns to hand out and give each child a penny. Pause to say 'thank you' when a bun is purchased! One group made a felt-covered board in the design of a baker's shop and used velcro-backed buns to display on the 'shelves'.

Support
Pair younger or differently-abled children with a helper so that they can still be included fully.

Extension
There is a wealth of counting rhymes available. Keep them simple, for example, only going up to three at first and gradually building up to five or higher. If you are starting at five, invite the children to 'show me five' first by holding up a hand with fingers splayed.

Follow-up ideas
- Play a partner hand game: 'Give me five, on the side, in the air, down below' etc.
- For children at a very early stage, start with

> *Two little dickey birds sitting on the wall,*
> *One called Peter, the other called Paul,*
> *Fly away Peter, fly away Paul,*
> *Come back Peter, come back Paul.*
>   (traditional)

- This last rhyme adapts beautifully to your own versions:

> *Two little fishes swimming in a tank*
> *One called Elsie, one called Frank,*
> *Swim away Elsie, swim away Frank,*
> *Swim back Elsie, swim back Frank* (etc.)

Activity 8.3   Nose, nose, show me your nose

Skill: To point to named body parts.
Target link: V5 V6 U2 A1 A7
Early Learning Goal link: CLL 1b, 1d and 4a
Birth to Three Framework link: stc1, stc2, skc1, skc3, skc4

What to do
You can easily make up your own verses which emphasise key words for children who might have difficulties in understanding them, or in selecting them out from long strings of words. These words were made up by parents and professionals in our child development centre group because we found that most action songs made the key words easy to miss. The tune is written out in a similar form to that used on page 24.

*Nose, nose,   show me your **nose**,*
G – – |C – – |G E   C |D –
The colder it is the more it blows!
D| C C C |D E F |E – D |C – –

Before each verse stop to invite all the children to point to the body part mentioned, prompting any children who need it. Repeat with other verses such as:

Ear, ear, show me an ear,
They hold on my specs and they help me to hear!
and
*Tummy, tummy, show me your **tummy**,*
I'll give it a tickle and make it feel funny! (etc.)

Support
This activity is suitable for even your youngest children.

Extension
Make up your own verses together. Here is one a group of parents made up earlier:

*Mouth, mouth, show me your **mouth**,*
Your hair's up north and your mouth's down south!

In one sense, it does not matter if you have a grown-up chuckle on the detail so long as the key words are emphasised and paused on.

Follow-up ideas
- Look for other songs and action rhymes with body parts in them.
- Use the *Everybody copy* rhyme (page 27) to copy pointing to different body parts.
- Play a game seeing what sounds the children can make with their hands and their feet.

Activity 8.4   Goldilocks

Skill: To listen and respond to a simple story-song.
Target link: G3 V1 V6 A1 A7
Early Learning Goal link: CLL 1b, 1d and 4a; MD 3a
Birth to Three Framework link: skc2, skc3, skc4, cl1, cl2

What to do
This song provides a wealth of learning opportunities for different ages and stages. You will find the song in *Okki-tokki-unga*. If you find singing difficult, you can speak this as a rhyme, but you will have to work a little harder to hold their interest. Alternatively, start the activity by telling the children a simple version of this familiar fairy tale.

The children will be most interested if you arrange some props. For example, you can have three different sized teddy bears, three chairs, three bowls, three toy beds of equivalent sizes. Steady the song up at the end of each verse as you count: 'One . . . two . . . three'.

To keep this song simple when working with children of mixed ability, I usually keep the same three actions for 'huge', 'small' and 'tiny', starting with my arms wide apart and ending with my hands close together. If you are telling the story instead of singing the song, use the same hand actions as you come to the appropriate parts of the story.

Encourage the children to match the props to the right bear as the story or song progresses, so that they have to think carefully about size.

Support
Use hand-over-hand to help the child sign 'huge', 'small' etc.

Extension
Play with differently sized bears, bowls, chairs and shoe box beds, encouraging the child to grade and match sizes. Support this by encouraging correct vocabulary.

Follow-up ideas
Have a music session based on bears (or other 'cuddlies') and invite each child to bring along their particular favourite. Select teddies to join in this song. Use the teddies to 'sing' *Miss Polly had a dolly* (traditional), to point to body parts, to rock for *Rock-a-bye baby* or *Row, row, row the boat* etc.

Activity 8.5   This is the way

Skill: To think about sequences of actions.
Target link: G3 V5 V6 A7
Early Learning Goal link: CLL 2a; KUW 5b; PD 1a
Birth to Three Framework link: stc1, skc1, skc3, skc4, hc1, hc4

What to do
Tell the children you are going to sing a song all about getting up in the morning. What do the children do when they wake? Prompt replies such as: 'get out of bed', 'wash my face', 'brush my teeth', 'have my breakfast', 'put on my clothes', 'go to playgroup' etc.

Now build their answers into a 'getting up song', using the tune of *Here we go round the mulberry bush*. Ask the children for ideas about how to mime each action, then sing the song together. Here is one example:

> *This is the way I get out of bed . . .*
> *This is the way I wash my face . . .*
> *This is the way I pull on my tee-shirt . . .*
> *This is the way I eat my toast . . .*
> *This is the way I brush my teeth . . .* etc.

You can make this into a movement game by joining hands and moving round as you sing *Here we go round the mulberry bush* (. . . on a cold and frosty morning) between each verse.

Support
Share simple photographs of each action with a child as you sing the verse.

Extension
Invent a similar song about your pre-school, inviting ideas from the children about activities and mimed actions to build in to it, telling all about their day there.

Follow-up ideas
- If you listen to children's song tapes and look through your resources, you will find other songs about sequences of actions.
- Use action picture cards for the children to place in the correct order – getting up, going downstairs, eating breakfast, putting on a coat etc.

Activity 8.6   Voices

Skill: To learn to control the tone and volume of their voices to request.
Target link: G4 S1 S5 A2
Early Learning Goal link: CLL 1c and 1f; CD 2a
Birth to Three Framework link: stc1, stc2, skc2, skc3, skc4

What to do
This is a helpful game to help children control the volumes and tones of their voices. The leader asks the questions and the children reply in different tones of voice. The style of voice can then be referred to later in the day in the group or at home in order to help the child develop different 'voices'.

Have you got your quiet voices?
Yes we have, we really have!

HAVE YOU GOT YOUR LOUD VOICES?
YES WE HAVE, WE REALLY HAVE!

Have you got your whiny voices?
Yes we have, we really have!

Have you got your cross voices?
Yes we have, we really have!

Have you got your happy voices?
Yes we have, we really have!'

Support
This activity is excellent for helping children who have autistic spectrum difficulties and who have already developed language to learn how to control their voice levels and tones.

Extension
Let an older child lead and think of new verses.

Follow-up ideas
Consider teaching children about their 'indoor voices' and their 'outdoor voices' and help them learn which is appropriate to use and when.

Activity 8.7   The music man

Skill: To learn the words of the musical instruments.
Target link: L3 L4 V6 A7
Early Learning Goal link: PSE 1b; KUW 2a; PD 4a and 5a; CD 2a
Birth to Three Framework link: skc1, skc2, skc3, skc4, cl2, cl3

What to do
Start by introducing *The Music Man* song and actions which you will find in
Okki-tokki-unga. Then try this variation.

Leader:	I am the music man, I come from down your way, and I can play . . .
Children:	What can you play?
Leader:	I play the *triangle*.

Now pick up a triangle, ask the children to repeat its name, and show them how you play it. Show how it makes a horrible sound if you hold the metal. Say how clever it is to dangle it by the string and what a good sound it makes if you then strike it. Let the children sing the chorus as you play the triangle. Now repeat for other instruments, choosing three or four to demonstrate each time.

Support
Let younger children play with the instruments on a separate occasion so that you can show them how to make the best sounds with them. The novelty will then have worn off sufficiently for them to give you their best attention during the group.

Extension
Bring in other musical instruments (and their players!) so that the children can hear new musical sounds.

Follow-up ideas
- You can use this activity as part of band time too, inviting just the tambourines to play for one verse, or just the drums for another, whilst you all sing the words.
- Provide an activity sheet with a picture of all your instruments and invite your children to colour in the different instruments they have played each session until gradually the sheet is completely coloured in. This is one way of encouraging the children to try different instruments and not always the same favourites.
- Sing *We can play on the big bass drum* (from *Okki-tokki-unga*).

Activity 8.8   This old man

Skill: To listen to and think of rhyming words.
Target link: V1 V5 V6 M1 M5 S1 S8 A5
Early Learning Goal link: CLL 1b, 1d, 3b and 4a
Birth to Three Framework link: skc1, skc2, skc3, cl1

What to do
Research has suggested that children who can hear rhymes in words and syllables may be less likely to have specific difficulties in reading letter sounds later on. Much of your rhyming and singing will be helping this skill. You can also adapt a familiar rhyming song by asking the children to fill in missing words. This tune is likely to be familiar to you:

> *This old man, he played one,*
> *He played nick-nack on my . . .*

At this stage, stop and invite the children to think of a rhyming word to go with 'one'. They will find this very hard at first, so you might need to suggest words yourself until the children tell you that the two words sound the same:
'One . . . pot'; 'one . . . umbrella'; 'one . . . bun', etc. Make it obvious for them (if you get some silly or rude answers, do not flinch, but ask for another word instead).

Finish each verse with the chorus:

> *With a nick-nack-paddywack, give a dog a bone,*
> *this old man came rolling home.*

Provide a repetitive action for any non-verbal children to join in during the chorus, a bounce on a knee, a clapping or a rolling action. Continue with higher numbers – up to four or five.

Support
Even the older babies can join in the 'rolling home' if their carer crosses their arms, holds their baby's hands gently and makes a roly poly action.

Extension
You can introduce 'pause-and-rhyme' to many different nursery rhymes and action songs.

Follow-up ideas
- Look for other action rhymes which enable the children to think of their own words, for example, 'When I was one, I ate a bun'.
- You will find other activities to teach basic concepts such as high/low, up/down, loud/quiet, quick/slow in Chapters 7 and 9.

Chapter 9

Band time

Children find the musical instruments particularly motivating. Keep them to one side (away from distraction) until you are ready for the children to choose. Ask them to choose one for their grown-ups too. Here are eight activities to encourage children or families to learn together as they enjoy joining in with their instruments. You will find a tape recorder or CD player and selection of recordings useful if you do not have access to live music.

Activity 9.1   Join the band

Skill: To join in with musical instruments, starting and stopping when the leader does.
Target link: G1 G2 G3 G4 L1 L3 L4 V2 V5 V6 A1 A7 I1 I2 I3 I5 I6 I8
Early Learning Goal link: CLL 1b; PD 5a; CD 2a and 3a
Birth to Three Framework link: stc2, stc3, stc4, skc3, cl3

What to do
This is the best warm-up for band time. It is best to keep band time until the end of the session, say, the last ten minutes. This is because the children usually find this activity the most enjoyable and they would be disappointed to have to put the instruments away and resume action songs afterwards. Instead, use it as the climax of your session. When children are particularly fretful or inattentive, you can move into band time sooner and have a shorter session, ending on a successful 'note'.

Put the musical instruments (see Chapter 1) in a box and place it in the centre of the circle. Invite each child to come and choose an instrument for themselves. If you have more than ten children, you might like to name children to come forwards to choose so that everyone is not taking at once. Make sure children with particular needs also make a personal choice wherever possible; do not restrict them by selecting what you wish them to play. Make sure all the adults have an instrument too.

Invite the children to watch you: 'When I play, you play too. When I stop, you stop too'. Put on your musical cassette/CD or start to play your instrument. After a minute or so, stop and look around the faces. Praise children by name for looking and listening. Repeat this three or four times, perhaps 'catching them out' with a very short passage at the end.

Support
Use a gentle physical prompt to stop the child playing when the music does and focus the child's attention on the listener.

Extension
Older children can lead the starting and stopping themselves. Watch them start and stop their instrument and operate the CD/cassette player accordingly.

Follow-up idea
- This basic activity helps the children to look and listen. Once they are 'tuned in', you can move straight on to do up to two other band time activities within any one session.

Activity 9.2   Loudly and quietly

Skill: To play an instrument loudly or quietly in imitation.
Target link: G1 G2 G3 G4 L1 L3 L4 L7 V2 V5 V6 U9 A1 A7 I1 I2 I3 I5 I6 I8 I10
Early Learning Goal link: CLL 1b; PD 5a; CD 2a and 3a
Birth to Three Framework link: skc1, skc3, skc4, cl1

What to do
Once the children are starting and stopping in a controlled and attentive way, introduce a new challenge: 'I wonder who can play their instrument very quietly?' Take up a percussion instrument yourself and encourage everyone to play very quietly. Praise them for being so clever – it is much harder to play quietly than loudly. Now challenge them to play as loudly as possible. Warn quieter children first and allow them to put their hands over their ears.

Now introduce the main activity: 'When you hear the music playing very quietly, see if you can play quietly too. When you hear it playing loudly, you play loudly too. You will have to look and to listen very carefully'. Play passages of music, each a minute or so long. Vary the loudness from two extremes – loud or very quiet. Praise the children by name, using the words you are teaching: 'Sultan, you are playing quietly' etc.

Support
With children who are very noise-sensitive, you are going to have to leave the really loud playing until they are more used to the group. Also, be conscious of any children with radio aids and hearing aids, taking care to avoid uncomfortable noises or volumes.

Extension
Certain older children will enjoy being successful leaders.

Follow-up ideas

- Once the children are familiar with this activity, see if they can accompany a longer passage of music which starts quietly, gets gradually louder, then becomes quiet again.

- Introduce a hand signal for loud (e.g. arms pushing upwards) and quiet (e.g. arms damping downwards) and invite a helper or older child to conduct you all.

Activity 9.3   Runaway train

Skill: To play an instrument fast or slow in imitation.
Target link: G1 G2 G3 G4 L1 L3 L4 L8 V2 V5 V6 S8 A1 A7 I1 I2 I3 I5 I6 I7 I8 I9
Early Learning Goal link: CLL 1b; PD 5a; CD 2a and 3a
Birth to Three Framework link: skc1, skc3, skc4, cl1, cl2

What to do
Introduce this activity in a similar way to the previous activity. First, make sure the children understand how to play 'fast' and 'slow', then build it into an activity.

Tell the children you are going to play some train music. Let's pretend that the steam train has stopped in the station: 'Is everybody on board? Are all the doors closed? Here comes the guard, and she's going to blow her whistle! Count with me . . . *one* . . . *two* . . . *three* . . .' Give one of your helpers a whistle to blow.

The best music for this is the country dance tune *Runaway train*, played on a tuned instrument, though other train-like music would suit. Start very slowly, and provide a running commentary to the children: 'We're pulling out of the station . . . getting faster . . . very fast . . . here comes a hill . . . I think I can, I think I can . . . over the hill and fast again . . . here comes a station . . . slowing down . . . slower . . . all stop!' (etc.) Repeat the whistle blowing when you start off again and repeat for two or three stations.

If you prefer, you can play this activity without music. Make sure you have a few adults or older children to provide a strong beat, taking their lead from your own percussion instrument. Include a strong drum, scratchy sounds, and shaking sounds to give the impression of a train in motion.

Support
Younger children will need to be helped and supported by a carer.

Extension
Make up other sound stories together.

Follow-up ideas
- Sit in a long line and pretend you are the carriages.
- Invite different children to be the guard and blow the whistle, particularly if you have a child who is just learning to blow. Use an antiseptic wipe for hygiene if you are passing the whistle between children.

Activity 9.4   Musical swaps

Skill: To encourage children to try a range of different percussion instruments.
Target link: G1 G2 G3 G4 L1 L3 L4 V2 V5 V6 A1 A7 I1 I2 I3 I5 I6 I8
Early Learning Goal link: CLL 1b; PD 5a; CD 2a and 3a
Birth to Three Framework link: skc1, skc3, cl3

What to do
Repeat the 'Join the Band' activity on page 58 and each time the music stops, encourage the children to try a different instrument. Pause while the adults check that each child knows how to play their choice, modelling how triangles are held in a position for the best sound; how hand drums are beaten with hands and snare drums with beaters; how cymbals need not catch noses; how indian bells are moved up and down against each other and not struck like cymbals etc.

Repeat for three or four instruments, changing round each time the music stops. This activity also works well if you have a large group and do not yet have enough instruments to go round all the children.

Support
You may have children who need to practise certain actions, perhaps following a programme from the physiotherapist or occupational therapist – ask parents to keep you informed. They might need to practise shaking, handling two objects at once, striking one object with another, or bringing a weak hand into use. Think about this creatively so that you can encourage the playing of instruments which are going to teach these skills.

Extension
Older children can 'compose' different sounds by helping you select which instruments should be played to each piece of music, for example, an assortment of bells for *Jingle Bells*.

Follow-up ideas
• Build this activity into the *Music Man* song (page 56) and use the activity sheet suggested on the same page.

Activity 9.5   Leading the band

Skill: To become confident enough to start and stop the whole band.
Target link: G1 G2 G3 G4 L1 L3 L4 V2 V5 V6 A1 A7 I1 I2 I3 I5 I6 I8 I11
Early Learning Goal link: PSE 1b; CLL 1b; PD 5a; CD 2a and 3a
Birth to Three Framework link: stc4, skc3, cl2, cl3, hc1

What to do
Once the children are used to the 'Join the Band' activity on page 58, exchange your role with one of the children. When they start to play, everyone starts to play. When they stop, everyone does. Have a supporting adult sitting alongside that child to encourage and prompt if necessary.

This works very well for children who have very little confidence, but is best done after four or five music sessions, when they are feeling secure. It also works well for the contrary child. Occasionally, one child starts to play as you stop and stops as you start! This is best tackled by ignoring the behaviour, at the same time praising by name the children who are co-operating with the aim of the activity. However, you can be pleasantly surprised if you then 'turn the tables', copying the starting and stopping of this child. Suddenly, you are all giving positive attention and the child is joining the new activity appropriately without even setting out to! There may be an initial crossness, then a big smile and a sense of pride in the influence s/he is having on all the others.

Support
This activity is also excellent for children with autistic or communication difficulties. They may not have found the action rhymes motivating, but are likely to enjoy the instruments. By encouraging the others to start playing when a certain child does and to stop when they do, you can sometimes see the point where a child 'in a world of their own' suddenly notes with delight that the whole group is mirroring them. You can then encourage several 'turn-takes' of playing as you copy and respond together.

Extension
Allow an older child to develop a simple system of conductor's signals, for example, for 'quietly' and 'loudly'.

Follow-up ideas
- Allow different children to lead the march, again starting and stopping the entire proceedings.
- Give a child a drum to beat or a whistle to blow to signal 'start' and 'stop'.

Activity 9.6   Musical stories

Skill: To select sound effects for a familiar story.
Target link: L1 L6 A1 A2 I1 I2 I3 I4 I5 I6
Early Learning Goal link: PSE 3b; CLL 1b and 1d; PD 5a; CD 2a, 4a, 3a and 4b
Birth to Three Framework link: skc3, skc4, cl1, cl2, cl3

What to do
Choose a short story or story rhyme that the children are already very familiar with, for example, *Billy Goats Gruff, Three Little Pigs* or *Rapunzel*. Remind the children of the main story line. Now invite them to choose some sounds to go with the story.

Place a selection of instruments in the centre of the circle including other sources of sound effects, for example, crinkly paper, a washboard and wooden spoon, a thunder sheet, coconut shells, blowing tubes, steam train whistle etc. This works best in a small group.

Go over the story and encourage a discussion and experimentation so that the group can select the best sounds to go with the story. Make sure every child is included. Use an adult helper to prompt the children and encourage them to come in at the right time. Rehearse the whole story together and then tell it to the parents and carers at home time.

Support
Include the youngest children by choosing a simple sound for them to play.

Extension
Older children can make up their own musical stories.

Follow-up ideas
- Invite all the children to select instruments to make 'happy' music, 'cross' music, 'scary' music, 'sleepy' music etc.

- Look for opportunities for the children to use the musical instruments creatively and combine them in new and interesting ways. Always make sure each and every child has a role to play, even if they find it hard to think creatively themselves.

Activity 9.7   Watch the conductor

Skill: To look and respond to a hand signal.
Target link: G1 G2 G3 G4 L1 L3 L4 V2 V5 V6 A1 A7 I1 I2 I3 I5 I6 I8
Early Learning Goal link: CLL 1b; PD 5a; CD 2a and 3a
Birth to Three Framework link: stc4, skc1, skc3, cl3

What to do
This is an activity for children well used to the routines of the music session and well used to both looking and listening. In this activity, you choose the instruments that you would like the children to play. Give them out in sections so that all the children with shakers are next to each other, then the drums, then the jingle bells etc.

Tell the children that they will need to watch very carefully, because the conductor will show them when to start and when to stop. Introduce the two hand signals – a downwards arm movement for 'start' and a policeman's halt signal for 'stop'.

You can either be the conductor yourself, in which case you will need a helper to operate the tape or to play the accompaniment. Alternately, you provide the music but use a helper to conduct. Practise starting and stopping to the conductor's signal.

Now tell the children that the conductor will point to different groups of instruments and tell them when to start and stop. Start the tape or accompaniment and ask the conductor to signal to the drums, to the bells, to the shakers etc., when they are to join in and when they are to stop. Start by bringing the groups of instruments in gradually, have a central section with everyone taking part, then gradually fade the music as different sections drop out again. Praise the children for looking.

Support
Give younger children a soft sound that they can play continuously (a rattle perhaps) or pair them with a helper who will relay the signals to the younger children using modelling or hand-over-hand support.

Follow-up ideas
- This makes a good display for an open day or concert. Keep it relaxed and happy.
- Introduce other hand signals too to make this more challenging, for example, 'start', 'stop', 'loud', 'soft'.

Activity 9.8   Marching

Skill: To develop a one-two rhythm, and to move whilst playing an instrument.
Target link: G1 G2 G4 L3 L4 L6 V6 M1 M2 M4 M5 M6 U9 I1 I2 I3 I4 I5 I6 I8 I12
Early Learning Goal link: PSE 1b; CLL 1b; PD 1a and 5a; CD 2a, 3a and 4a
Birth to Three Framework link: stc4, skc1, skc3, cl3, hc2

What to do
Once children are confident within the sessions, this is a good activity to finish on.

Invite the children to choose an instrument they can carry, and to line up behind you. This should be voluntary, and children who prefer to can remain in the circle, contributing to the background music. Move around the outside of the circle, playing your own instrument as you go (or ask one of your helpers to work the tape). Encourage the children to march behind you, playing their instruments as they go. Stamp your feet and have a strong drum beat to emphasise the strong one-two rhythm of the march. Children learn rhythms best if they can move to them.

Every now and then, stop the music and turn round to see who is following you. Praise children by name for looking and listening well. Do not expect the little ones to stay in line – you are likely to find a rather general meandering and this is perfectly acceptable at this stage.

If you have the opportunity, prepare spaces ahead so that you can all move into other areas of the pre-school, or even outdoors if appropriate.

Support
Make sure that children who are non-ambulant have a chance to be wheeled or carried in the march if they want to.

Extension
Older children can lead as you play a version of *Follow my leader*, playing loudly and quietly, quickly and slowly in imitation of the leader.

Follow-up ideas
- Allow other children to lead the march from time to time.
- Use a march as part of your summer fete or a special celebration, to show off to the parents.
- Look for ways of making your instruments portable, for example, drums on straps which should go over a shoulder for safety.

Chapter 10

Snapshot of the Music Makers approach in action

In this chapter, there is an example of how the Music Makers approach was used to encourage children who had SEN to make progress within their local playgroup. You will be given a 'snapshot' of a setting so that you can visualise what a typical music session might look like.

In this particular model, the author used a training method to introduce settings to Music Makers. She visited the group on four consecutive weeks, each time doing slightly less as staff and parents did slightly more. Thus they learned how to 'go it alone', step by small step with support from a visiting musician and trainer. In this snapshot, it is the first training visit and the trainer is reflecting on the responses of the children and the adults she is leading.

Snapshot of Richie

First Music Makers session at a large 100-place town playgroup, with children in two large pre-fabricated huts according to their age. I am given the three-to-four year-olds; about thirty of them with four adults who do not look at all confident with the proceedings.

Richie is running around, shouting and jumping off the tables. He has recently been diagnosed as having Asperger's Syndrome. His parents are understandably upset and extremely tense. Perhaps partly for this reason, Richie's behaviour has almost been beyond control during the last few days. It is his father who has brought him today.

I start with a warm-up song. The children look happy and watch carefully. The adults still look unsure and do not sing. Richie is held on his Dad's knee and immediately goes into full struggle and scream, beating his father and shouting 'silly music'. We battle on. He escapes. I explain to his father that I would like to see him go his own way to see if I can attract him with the music. Dad tells me 'You'll be lucky'. We try again. The children are joining in with a clapping song, and the adults 'unfreezing'.

We sing the greeting song. Richie stops at his name and looks at me, smiling. He runs off again. We sing a wobbly jelly song. The children are now attending beautifully, with the exception of Richie. Merle has severe speech and language delay and is watching attentively, joining in the actions. Ben 'never sits still' and has attention difficulties; he is watching me closely and following the clues.

I lay the percussion instruments out on the floor, asking the children to wait until I have finished before choosing and, just as I am about to invite Richie to choose first, he darts in and grabs a drum and a stick. He takes it to a side table away from the group and is absorbed in beating it. We all play – I tell the children to play when I play and stop when I stop. We have a few goes. They all look and listen for my piano accordion attentively, even those with listening difficulties.

I then explain we will start when Richie starts and stop when Richie stops. After two goes of this, Richie looks up at me with a full and almost startling eye contact. He drums furiously and stops. We all join in loudly. He smiles. He gives one soft tap. We copy. He plays a long string. We copy. By this time, he is grinning and I feel in full reciprocal communication with him. He looks playful for a moment as he sees just how quiet he can be and we still hear him and copy. This carries on for a full four minutes. Richie is leading the band. Dad is smiling.

We start to march around Richie and his drum. When I halt, everyone stops and we do not start until Richie beats his drum again. This takes us to the end of the twenty minutes. Richie occasionally 'runs off some steam', but then returns to his drum.

Chapter 11

The evaluative research

This chapter briefly describes an evaluation of the Music Makers Approach carried out by the author as a piece of doctoral research at the University of Sheffield (2001). The aim of the original Music Makers project was to develop reflective practice in early years educators and to enable them to improve the developmental skills of any children who have SEN in their settings.

Fifty-four early years educators attached to 29 settings were trained in the approach and used the methods they had learned to target 49 children with SEN. Questionnaire data were collected to evaluate how early years educators were developing their practice following training. The developmental checklist shown on page 73 was designed, its reliability between observers checked, and used to measure changes in the children's skills. Thirty early years educators were interviewed six months after training and the transcripts analysed using research methods called 'content analysis' and 'Grounded Theory'.

All settings continued to use the Music Makers Approach twelve months after training. It was seen by them as increasing both their own and the children's confidence and as a useful way to encourage all the children to join in. Many reflected on the positive changes they had seen in all the children's motivation, behaviour and confidence and how this was also generalising to other learning situations.

There were 49 children each with very individual special educational needs and each attending very different settings with very different people. Inevitably, their rates of progress were individual and unique. Nevertheless, early years educators were left with the overwhelming impression that they had all made good progress across each area of the checklist (page 73). Progress was dependent on early years educators selecting appropriate activities to meet additional needs, and many of them felt more able to do this since using the Music Makers Approach.

The reasons early years educators gave for the children's progress were varied and again suggested much reflective thought about the effect they could have upon their children's learning. Many considered that progress was linked to the children's enjoyment of the music sessions, their better ability to look and to listen in this kind of approach, their response to the familiar routine, and their increased confidence.

The following theoretical model describing the relationships which exist when adults and children learn together began to emerge. When early years educators reflect carefully about their practice, they become better able to meet the additional needs of the children they are working with. This, in turn, enables them to see evidence of the children's progress and contribute further to encouraging and maintaining it. The more the children progress, the greater the confidence of the educator, and the more individually they become able to meet needs. The progress of the one affects the progress of the other as adult and child learn together.

Young children respond well to set structures and routines which enable them to anticipate and predict. This, in turn, seems to improve their confidence as learners, their ability to attend and their motivation to join in. With familiarity comes better attention, more appropriate behaviour, and more opportunities to learn.

However, set structures and routines also help the early years educator to develop her or his own skills and confidence, making them better able to deliver the curriculum with that level of flexibility and creativity needed to ensure that additional needs are met, moment by moment. Learning in both adults and children is therefore an ongoing process.

Practical 'how to do it' approaches enable early years educators to develop their skills and confidence. If such approaches 'work' in the sense that the children respond positively and make progress, then those approaches tend to be used long after the training period has ended. This enables further practice and development of skills which can then be generalised to new learning situations. It also allows any belief systems which have been strengthened by the approach (e.g. that 'inclusion works') to take root. Finally, it allows the early years educator to develop the skills and confidence needed to help the children generalise their progress to new situations.

With practice and confidence comes the ability of early years educators to develop new teaching styles and approaches. They become able to 'take risks' in leaving their regular routines in order to 'go with the child', the opportunity and the moment. In fact, they have developed the ability to think reflectively about what it is they can do to enhance the children's learning and plan their next approaches in light of this, not only in their planning but 'on the hoof' as well.

The Music Makers Approach has been successful in encouraging pre-school workers to think reflectively about their practice and to develop their approaches so as best to enhance the children's learning and progress. This is despite many of them having little previous experience or training. The success of the approach may be because it supports the interaction between adults and children, developing the skills and confidences of both and enabling the success of one to foster the success of the other. It may also be because it allows the learning process to be extended over time and leads to generalisation of skills from one area to another. Settings tend to continue to use the approach independently long after their training is completed.

It has also been shown to improve the developmental skills of children who have SEN, perhaps because it uses routines and builds confidence over time. However, early years educators have found it to be an approach for all children (not just those with SEN), and it has therefore proved to be a practical way of delivering the early years curriculum inclusively. This is why this present book (the second edition of the Music Makers manual) has focussed on Music Makers as a musical circle time approach for *everyone* and not only as an approach for including children who have SEN or additional needs.

Early Learning Goals

Reference numbers used in activity sheets

Personal, Social and Emotional Development

PSE 1	**Dispositions and attitudes**
PSE 1a	Continue to be interested, excited and motivated to learn
PSE 1b	Be confident to try new activities, initiate ideas and speak in a familiar group
PSE 1c	Maintain attention, concentrate, and sit quietly when appropriate
PSE 2	**Self-confidence and self-esteem**
PSE 2a	Respond to significant experiences, showing a range of feelings when appropriate
PSE 2b	Have a developing awareness of their own needs, views and feelings and be sensitive to the needs, views and feelings of others
PSE 2c	Have a developing respect for their own cultures and beliefs and those of other people
PSE 3	**Making relationships**
PSE 3a	Form good relationships with adults and peers
PSE 3b	Work as part of a group or class, taking turns and sharing fairly, understanding that there need to be agreed values and codes of behaviour for groups of people, including adults and children, to work together harmoniously
PSE 4	**Behaviour and self-control**
PSE 4a	Understand what is right, what is wrong, and why
PSE 4b	Consider the consequences of their words and actions for themselves and others
PSE 5	**Self-care**
PSE 5a	Dress and undress independently and manage their own personal hygiene
PSE 5b	Select and use activities and resources independently
PSE 6	**Sense of community**
PSE 6a	Understand that people have different needs, views, cultures and beliefs, which need to be treated with respect
PSE 6b	Understand that they can expect others to treat their needs, views, cultures and beliefs with respect

Communication, Language and Literacy

CLL 1	**Communication**
CLL 1a	Interact with others, negotiate plans and activities and take turns in conversation
CLL1b	Enjoy listening to and using spoken and written language, and readily turn to it in their play and learning
CLL 1c	Sustain attentive listening, responding to what they have heard by relevant comments, questions or actions
CLL 1d	Listen with enjoyment and respond to stories, songs and other music, rhymes and poems and make up their own stories, songs, rhymes and poems
CLL 1e	Extend their vocabulary, exploring the meanings and sounds of new words
CLL 1f	Speak clearly and audibly with confidence and control and show awareness of the listener, for example through their use of conventions such as greetings, 'please' and 'thank you'
CLL 2	**Thinking**
CLL 2a	Use language to imagine and recreate roles and experiences
CLL 2b	Use talk to organise, sequence and clarify thinking, ideas, feelings and events
CLL 3	**Sounds and letters**
CLL 3a	Hear and say initial and final sounds in words, and short vowel sounds within words
CLL 3b	Link sounds to letters, naming and sounding the letters of the alphabet

CLL 4	**Reading**
CLL 4a	Explore and experiment with sounds, words and texts
CLL 4b	Retell narratives in the correct sequence, drawing on the language patterns of stories
CLL 4c	Read a range of familiar and common words and simple sentences independently
CLL 4d	Know that print carries meaning and, in English, is read from left to right and top to bottom
CLL 4e	Show an understanding of the elements of stories, such as main characters, sequence of events, and openings, and how information can be found in non-fiction texts to answer questions about where, who, why and how
CLL 5	**Writing**
CLL 5a	Use their phonic knowledge to write simple regular words and make phonetically plausible attempts at more complex words
CLL 5b	Attempt writing for different purposes, using features of different forms such as lists, stories and instructions
CLL 5c	Write their own names and other things such as labels and captions and begin to form simple sentences, sometimes using punctuation
CLL 6	**Handwriting**
CLL 6a	Use a pencil and hold it effectively to form recognisable letters, most of which are correctly formed

Mathematical Development

MD 1	**Numbers and labels for counting**
MD 1a	Say and use number names in order in familiar contexts
MD 1b	Count reliably up to ten everyday objects
MD 1c	Recognise numerals 1 to 9
MD 1d	Use developing mathematical ideas and methods to solve practical problems
MD 2	**Calculating**
MD 2a	In practical activities and discussion begin to use the vocabulary involved in adding and subtracting
MD 2b	Use language such as 'more' or 'less' to compare two numbers
MD 2c	Find one more or one less than a number from 1 to 10
MD 2d	Begin to relate addition to combining two groups of objects and subtraction to 'taking away'
MD 3	**Shape, space and measure**
MD 3a	Use language such as 'greater', 'smaller', 'heavier' or 'lighter' to compare quantities
MD 3b	Talk about, recognise, and recreate simple patterns
MD 3c	Use language such as 'circle' or 'bigger' to describe the shape and size of solids and flat shapes

Knowledge and Understanding of the World

KUW 1	**Exploration and investigation**
KUW 1a	Investigate objects and materials by using all of their senses as appropriate
KUW 1b	Find out about, and identify some features of, living things, objects and events they observe
KUW 1c	Look closely at similarities, differences, patterns and change
KUW 1d	Ask questions about why things happen and how things work
KUW 2	**Designing and making skills**
KUW 2a	Build and construct with a wide range of objects, selecting appropriate resources, and adapting their work where necessary
KUW 2b	Select the tools and techniques they need to shape, assemble and join the materials they are using

KUW 3	**Information and communication technology**
KUW 3a	Find out about and identify the uses of everyday technology and use information and communication technology and programmable toys to support their learning
KUW 4	**A sense of time**
KUW 4a	Find out about past and present events in their own lives, and in those of their families and other people they know
KUW 5	**A sense of place**
KUW 5a	Observe, find out about, and identify features in the place they live and the natural world
KUW 5b	Find out about their environment, and talk about those features they like and dislike
KUW 6	**Culture and beliefs**
KUW 6a	Begin to know about their own cultures and beliefs and those of other people

Physical Development

PD 1	**Movement**
PD 1a	Move with confidence, imagination and in safety
PD 1b	Move with control and coordination
PD 1c	Travel around, under, over and through balancing and climbing equipment
PD 2	**Sense of space**
PD 2a	Show awareness of space, of themselves and of others
PD 3	**Health and bodily awareness**
PD 3a	Recognise the importance of keeping healthy and those things which contribute to this
PD 3b	Recognise the changes that happen to their bodies when they are active
PD 4	**Using equipment**
PD 4a	Use a range of small and large equipment
PD 5	**Using tools and materials**
PD 5a	Handle tools, objects, construction and malleable materials safely and with increasing control

Creative Development

CD 1	**Exploring media and materials**
CD 1a	Explore colour, texture, shape, form and space in two and three dimensions
CD 2	**Music**
CD 2a	Recognise and explore how sounds can be changed, sing simple songs from memory, recognise repeated sounds and sound patterns and match movements to music
CD 3	**Imagination**
CD 3a	Use their imagination in art and design, music, dance, imaginative and role play and stories
CD 4	**Responding to experiences, and expressing and communicating ideas**
CD 4a	Respond in a variety of ways to what they see, hear, smell, touch and feel
CD 4b	Express and communicate their ideas, thoughts and feelings by using a widening range of materials, suitable tools, imaginative and role play, movement, designing and making, and a variety of songs and musical instruments

Birth to three matters framework

Reference numbers used in activity sheets

A Strong Child

stc1   Me, Myself and I (knowing who I am)
stc2   Being Acknowledged and Affirmed (including friendships)
stc3   Developing Self-assurance (including confidence)
stc4   A Sense of Belonging (becoming a member of a social group)

A Skilful Communicator

skc1   Being Together (communication)
skc2   Finding a Voice (language expression)
skc3   Listening and Responding (language reception)
skc4   Making Meaning (both comprehension and early literacy)

A Competent Learner

cl1   Making Connections (making sense, finding out and early maths)
cl2   Being Imaginative
cl3   Being Creative (movement and touch, music and art and craft)
cl4   Representing (including early mark-making)

A Healthy Child

hc1   Emotional Well-being (including self-help)
hc2   Growing and Developing (including physical development and feeding)
hc3   Keeping Safe
hc4   Healthy Choices (including personal hygiene)

These categories appear in more detail in *Trackers 0–3* published by QEd Publications.

Music Makers

Name of child: _____   Group: _____

Name of observer: _____

In the Initial Assessment column – enter one tick if s/he can do that skill sometimes, and two ticks if s/he can do that skill almost always.

In the Target Skill column – tick skills you would really like her/him to learn in the music group during the next term.

Activity	Initial Assessment Date:	Target Skill	Final Assessment Date:
G: General			
1. Stops fretting during music			
2. Enjoys music			
3. Joins in group on parent's knee			
4. Begins to join in independently			
L: Listening			
1. Turns towards a sound			
2. Recognises familiar tunes			
3. Starts playing when leader does			
4. Stops playing when leader does			
5. Finds familiar voice from choice of two			
6. Imitates simple rhythm with prompt			
7. Plays loudly/quietly in imitation			
8. Plays quickly/slowly in imitation			
V: Looking			
1. Turns to look at person singing			
2. Turns from one sound to another			
3. Gives eye contact when greeted			
4. Looks towards a hidden sound			
5. Watches other children			
6. Looks at group leader occasionally			
M: Movement			
1. Allows self to be bounced on knee			
2. Makes general movements to music			
3. Allows arms to be moved to music			
4. Allows legs to be moved to music			
5. Bounces when held in standing position			
6. Dances/moves independently to music			
7. Moves fast/slow to different music			

Activity	Initial Assessment Date:	Target Skill	Final Assessment Date:
S: Singing & vocalising			
1. Makes general sounds to music			
2. Makes tuneful sounds to music			
3. Tries to sing familiar songs			
4. Joins in animal sounds			
5. Joins in repeated sounds, b - b etc.			
6. Joins in key words, e.g. 'down'			
7. Says familiar phrases, e.g. 'e - i - e - i- o'			
8. Counts to three			
U: Understanding			
1. Turns to his/her name			
2. Points to one or two body parts			
3. Points to several body parts			
4. Responds to up/down			
5. Responds to high/low			
6. Responds to loud/quiet			
7. Points to some named colours			
8. Shows me five fingers			
9. Understands 'look', 'listen'			
A: Actions			
1. Allows self to be prompted			
2. Demonstrates awareness of what comes next			
3. Claps hands to request			
4. Waves bye bye in imitation			
5. Joins in clapping song			
6. Moves hands for high/low			
7. Copies new actions			
I: Instruments			
1. Holds a shaking instrument when placed in hand			
2. Can shake instrument			
3. Copies a hand beat on tambourine			
4. Holds two things at once			
5. Beats two parts of instrument together			
6. Beats drum with stick			
7. Blows instrument			
8. Joins in the band			
9. Plays fast/slow to different music			
10. Plays quiet/loud to different music			
11. Leads the band			
12. Marches and plays at same time			

Music Makers

Session planning sheet

Activity	Date	Leader	Targets
Warm-up Chapters 4 and 7			
Greeting song Chapter 4			
Action rhymes Chapters 7 and 8			
Looking and listening game Chapter 5			
Movement Chapter 6			
Spoken rhyme Chapters 5, 6, 7 and 8			
Band time Chapter 9			
Goodbye song Chapter 4			

References and useful resources

References

Allen, T. (2004) *Accelerating Babies' Communication*. Stafford: QEd Publications.

DfES (2001) *The Special Educational Needs Code of Practice*. Nottingham: DfES Publications.

Harrop, B., Friend, L. and Gadsby, D. (1975) *Okki-tokki-unga: Action Songs for Children*. London: A & C Black.

Matterson, E. (Ed) (2004) *This Little Puffin*. London: Puffin Books.

Mortimer, H. (2001) *A study to evaluate how the Music Makers Approach can be used as a training method to develop reflective practice in pre-school workers in the voluntary and private sectors*. EdD Thesis, University of Sheffield.

Mortimer, H. (2003) *Trackers 0-3*. Stafford: QEd Publications.

Mortimer, H. (2005) *Step by Step: Helping parents and carers support young children's development*. Stafford: QEd Publications.

Mortimer, H. (2005) *RUMPUS: Planning behaviour groups for parents and carers of young children*. Stafford: QEd Publications.

Mortimer, H. (2005) *Music and Play: Introducing parents and carers of young children to working in groups*. Stafford: QEd Publications.

Mortimer, H. (2005) *Baby and Me: Planning support groups for new parents and their babies*. Stafford: QEd Publications.

Mortimer, H. (2006) *Making Connections: Promoting attachments between parents and carers and their young children*. Stafford: QEd Publications.

Pavelko, V. and Scott, L.B. (1976) *Apusskidu: Songs for Children*. London: A & C Black.

Rosen, M. and Oxenbury, H. (1989) *We're Going on a Bear Hunt*. London: Walker Books.

Useful resources

Early Learning Centre for tapes, instruments and song books.
Tel: 08705 352352
Website: www.elc.co.uk

LDA, Duke Street, Wisbech, Cambridgeshire PE13 2AE
Tel: 0845 120 4776
Website: www.ldalearning.com

Music Education Supplies Ltd, 101 Banstead Road South, Sutton, Surrey SM2 5LH

NESArnold for musical instruments and props.
Tel: 0845 120 4525
Website: www.nesarnold.co.uk

Step by Step (SBS) for colourful and more unusual musical instruments suitable for early years and SEN.
SBS, Lee Fold, Hyde, Cheshire SK14 4LL
Tel: 0845 3001089
Website: www.sbs-educational.co.uk

For information on Music Makers training:
Occasionally the author knows of seminars and workshops on Music Makers that are currently being run. Information on courses can be obtained on the QEd website at the following address
www.qed.uk.com/hannahm.htm